Other nonfiction books by Julian Serles

Here, Hold My Chicken!

KNOCK KNOCK! It's Carmack!

Build Your Dream!

Ax Minster and the Culinary Pleasures!

Other fiction books by Julian Serles

Girls, Inc.

Cover Photo: Proving that graffiti is all lies! At the start of the Cross Marin Trail, Olema, CA.

This book is dedicated to my stoker,
for whom I am always breaking wind.

Contents

I had a dream   1

Who wants to ride a tandem, anyway?   2

What do tandems have to do, have to do with it?   4
Divorce court   4
Strong play   4
Fast twitch   4

Set up for success   5
Enjoy the ride   5
T R U S T, tell you what it means to me   6
This is your captain speaking   7
Ten-four good buddy   8
     Captain says!   9
     Stoker says!   10
     All play   10

Let's get this party started   13
Who's on first?   13
Beg, borrow, or steal   14
Different strokes   14
I lean, you lean, we lean   15

In the beginning   17
One size does not fit all   17
To clip or not to clip, that is the question   18
The captain has turned on the "No Stopping!" sign   19
     Rubber-side down   19
     In captain I trust   21
     Trust is a two-way street   23

Attention on deck   24
It ain't easy being green   24
All dressed up   25

Tandemachina	**26**
Tour de beach	26
Tour de road	27
Burley Duet	28
Tour de gravel	31
Co-Motion Java	34
Tour de mountain	36
KHS Tandemania	38
Ventana El Conquistador de Montańas	42
Bigfoot down	45
New Bigfoot rising	46
Buy high, sell low	**48**
If the bike does not fit, you must acquit	48
Used tandem superstore	49
Bittersweet tandem sales	50
The new shiny	52
Order up	54
Wide load	**56**
Coupling couplers	57
Turning it up to 11	**60**
Tandem SMASH!	60
Stand and deliver	61
Traffic cop	62
You turn me right 'round baby	63

Two-way street	65
Up, up, and away	66
Rubber-side up	66
Parts is parts	**68**
Easy is the road	68
What a drag	68
Steep is the mountain	70
Boom goes the hub	70
Component musings	71
Maintenance schedule	71
Split ends	72
Ticket to ride	**77**
17 Mile Drive (road)	77
Fort Ord National Monument (mountain)	78
Point Reyes Lighthouse (road)	79
Irvine Regional Park (mountain)	80
Ventura River Trail (road)	80
Point Mugu State Park (mountain)	81
Coastside Trail (gravel grinder)	83
Mark Twain National Forest (mountain)	86
Newbury Park Surf Loop (gravel grinder)	88
Cross Marin Trail (gravel grinder)	90

I had a dream

The first time I sat on a bicycle, I was six years old and starting the first grade of elementary school. Even though I did not receive the best (or, not to put too fine a point on it, any) instruction and my first minute on my first bike ride was mostly spent picking myself off the ground after T-boning a neighbor's parked car, it was very clear what mastering the bicycle meant.

It meant freedom.

Once I started staying on my bike, I made friends who also had bikes. I made friends at the local BMX jumps. I rode my bike to school. I rode my bike to get out of the house. I rode my bike to the arcade. I rode my bike to deliver newspapers. I rode my bike to college. I rode my bike for exercise. I ride my bike to work.

Once I started driving I never stopped riding, but most of my friends did. After many years, many schools, and many moves, I had lost connections to other people that liked to ride bikes. I started to dream of having a tandem and someone to ride it with.

Through the looking glass of The Nest at Olema Cottages. (left)

It was a pretty vague dream; I think at that time I had not even seen a "real" tandem (and had absolutely no concept of a mountain tandem), only associating the word with the beach cruiser-style rental tandems seen along beach boardwalks the world over. That did not matter – it was not really about the bike. It was about finding a soul mate who just wanted to go ride bikes with me.

Looking back, it is strange to me that my dream involved a tandem specifically. Why not two riders on two single bikes? I obviously had no idea what it was like to be part of a tandem team. While this was not a fierce, recurring dream, it was in the back of my head, constantly, but softly.

At age 29 I was introduced to a woman who also liked to ride bikes. Our first date was a bike ride interrupted by a mechanical failure. Having walked back to her truck and driven to the local bike shop to get it repaired, I hoped she still wanted to do our ride. Luckily, she was hoping I still wanted to do our ride.

Strangely, that experience barely ticked my tandem dream. As the months and the rides piled up, however, the tandem dream started to sing loud. I do not remember discussing with my then-girlfriend buying a tandem, but about a year after we were introduced we were riding around the local bike shop testing a **Burley Duet** road tandem. Since we had not crashed 'round the block, it seemed like an excellent idea to buy it and make my dream come true.

It is impossible to have any regrets about that fateful purchase, and it is only after a dozen years of tandeming that I have enough experience and knowledge to write this book. Looking back, even after 23 years of riding single bikes, what I did not know about tandems was everything there was to know about riding tandem. The following pages will hopefully help you and your partner decide if you might want to pop down to the local bike shop and take a tandem for a spin…

Who wants to ride a tandem, anyway?

In **I had a dream** I mentioned it was strange to me that my dream involved a tandem. Someone to ride bikes with? Sure; but what specifically about a tandem made the dream better? I had no idea, but, for once, it turned out I was right about it anyway.

Riding tandem is enjoying the freedom of riding bikes while doing it with your partner (see **Who's on first** for more information about captains and stokers). Riding tandem is such a different experience compared to riding together on single bikes, and the reason is obvious. When riding single bikes you are only responsible for your own self and your own bike. When you ride tandem, you are riding as a team.

Riding as a team means you and your partner conquer the climbs together, conquer trail obstacles together, experience the ride together. On a single bike, summiting a road climb or cleaning a rock garden is a solo achievement. On a tandem, every movement is teamwork.

Now, maybe you are still locked into bike riding as freedom, and to you that freedom includes being free of everyone else. But how much better would the ride be if you could have your partner along, contributing to your mutual success? Also, think about how much easier it is to go for a ride when you do not have to convince your partner to let you out of the house. If your partner is a de facto part of the ride, you are no longer getting away but moving together.

Overlooking Monterey Bay is a great place for a stop after climbing Aptos Creek Fire Road in The Forest of Nisene Marks State Park. (right)

What do tandems have to do, have to do with it?

Divorce court

If you have found your way to this book and the subject of tandems, no doubt you have heard many people proclaim tandems as "divorce machines." This is a knee-jerk reaction by people who, in the main, have not ridden tandem, so let us get this myth out of the way early on.

Tandems are no more divorce machines than Ski Doos, Sony Playstations, or Mazda Miatas. None of those things, or a tandem, would cause relational strife that was not already there. If you are not communicating before getting on a tandem, however, the tandem experience will expose the lack of communication more fully.

Strong play

So tandems themselves cannot overcome communication issues. Tandems can, however, help compensate for teams in which one rider is stronger than the other. With the stronger rider captaining the front of the bike, the stoker can ride longer distances and tackle more challenging terrain. This can lead to significant improvement in the weaker rider's endurance, leading to longer rides over time.

At the same time, there is no guarantee tandem riding will convert a non-rider. If your partner is not a cyclist and does not have much interest in being a cyclist, sticking him or her on the back of a tandem is unlikely to change their view. You do not have to have the same skill and strength as your partner, but you both do have to have the desire to be on the bike.

Fast twitch

Tandems are also good for combining the strengths of a fast-twitch rider with those of a slow-twitch rider. When my then-girlfriend and I went for a ride on single bikes in early days, I would start out fast and, keeping to my normal pace, would be far ahead during the first half of the ride. After my partner had warmed up (slowly, but warmed up nonetheless), she would catch up and then be leading me at the end of the ride as I led her at the beginning.

Tandems help equalize the power outputs. Of course, fast-twitch people need to allow their slow-twitch partners to warm up, but the warm-up period can be shortened, and you are never leaving your partner behind. Towards the end of the ride the slow-twitch partner can provide a little more of the power while the fast-out-of-the-gate partner still has some in reserve.

Set up for success

The subsections that follow will discuss keys to becoming a successful tandem team. However, this entire section can be summed up in one word: trust. When people see us out on the bike and talk to us about riding tandem, my stoker almost always says some version of "I would not ride behind anyone else."

Of course, trust is a bigger part of the stoker's belief system – it has to be! The stoker has no control (brakes, gears, steering), but a stoker should need no control. The stoker should feel perfectly at ease on the back of the bike, and enabling the stoker to trust and feel at ease is the captain's job. A captain needs to trust the stoker as well, however. It is very much a two-way street.

Enjoy the ride

One key to enjoying riding tandem is to already enjoy riding single. Trying to convince someone who does not ride to give up control may seem like an easy task. And it may well be. However, there is no "I" in "team" and if you are not acting as a team on a tandem then you are about to crash. No one is born a rider, but those people who demonstrate a lack of interest in cycling and are only on the back of the bike because they were cajoled into the role probably will not form the core of a successful tandem team.

Conversely, it is not an easy task to convince someone who has controls on their single bike to give those up for the back seat on a tandem. That potential stoker, however, is someone who already rides, perhaps for some of the same reasons stated in **I have a dream**. Someone who enjoys the ride already could be more easily persuaded to the benefits of riding tandem as discussed in **Who wants to ride a tandem, anyway?**

Just because your potential captain or stoker does not currently like to ride, or perhaps does not ride at all, does not mean you will never ride tandem. This section is not written to dissuade you from trying – this book is all about riding together! However, beginning your persuasion with a tandem purchase should be avoided. Start on single bikes and warm up your partner to the joy of riding. Then start wondering aloud how great it would be to team up on a tandem.

T R U S T, tell you what it means to me

Stokers have no control of the tandem yet they are the key to it working properly. That may seem like hyperbole, but just imagine trying to captain a tandem with a stoker that was jerking about, or not pedaling, or pedaling too much. At best, any of those situations would result in an unpleasant ride.

While stokers, of course, have every intention of being a model team partner, assuming the position on the back of a tandem is generally not a natural experience. It takes time to get used to riding without control. It takes more time to trust your captain that he or she will have you in mind at all times. Trust me, we do. See **In captain I trust**.

Stokers cannot see what is coming up ahead; captains block 30°-40° of the straight-ahead from a stoker's view.

What a stoker sees from the back of a tandem. (left)

This is generally the bigger stumbling block for a new stoker than a lack of controls. If you cannot see what is ahead you do not know what is ahead and you cannot prepare for it. To a certain extent, it is riding blind, and it can be a huge issue.

Each tandem team will work out what needs to be communicated between captain and stoker. A captain will gain stoker trust by sharing the road or trail conditions (see **Ten-four good buddy**), giving back some "vision" to the stoker. A captain will also gain stoker trust by accommodating stoker requests for slower speeds or less-adventurous lines. As a team, you may well get to the point where you are running 45 mph downhill on a paved road (or, ahem, on a dirt fireroad). But pay careful attention to your stoker as you work up to those sorts of speeds as you will never get there if the stoker bails off the team because trust was not established or maintained.

This is your captain speaking

Captains have the most control of the tandem. Captains have brakes, gears, steering, and captains have a view ahead. Captains cannot forget, however, that what is behind is the most important thing: your stoker. Stoker trust is really the only thing that keeps a tandem team riding, so foremost amongst your responsibilities is to do no harm.

You should avoid doing anything that will spook the stoker. Things that spook stokers include not knowing about important and changing conditions ahead (low branches, traffic, bumps in the road). In addition to communicating road or trail conditions, let your stoker know what you need from your partner so they are not only aware but feel a part of the team.

It is up to the captain to choose proper lines (off-road or on) so that your stoker is not scared by speed, traffic, exposure (read: cliffs), etc. While riding tandem is a team endeavor, the specific line or route is decided by the captain.

Avoiding stoker anxiety is crucial in the early stages of learning to ride as a team, but it is also very important when your riding levels differ. For a captain with years of riding experience, perhaps that 45 mph downhill run on a curvy mountain road is a thrill; for the stoker on the back who might not have ridden faster than 15 mph on a single bike, 45 mph might as well be 700 mph! You as captain may have full control of the bike, clipping apexes like Mario Andretti, and the road may be free of traffic, but none of that matters to your stoker.

The same idea applies off-road. A quick little g-out or kicker is always fun, even on a tandem, except when you are unaware or unfamiliar. A stoker's first g-out on a tandem should be ridden with full notice beforehand and an agreed speed. This might be much slower than the captain would prefer, but it is also quite likely that your stoker will then request you turn around and hit it again. This time faster!

Your goal is to have a giggling stoker. As a captain, if you are hearing giggles from behind you, you are doing a superb job.

Ten-four good buddy

As mentioned in **What do tandems have to do with it?** and **T R U S T, tell you what it means to me**, communication when riding tandem is key. What you ride (on-road or off) will influence your communication needs, and each tandem team will have their own methods of communicating. Most communication is verbal (as opposed to physical) and, at times verbal communication can be difficult. This is mostly a factor of speed, as wind noise swallows words spoken just a few feet away. Wind noise is an issue at anything above 15 mph or so, and higher speeds make it more difficult for the captain to pull his eyes to turn around and speak to the stoker directly.

For verbal communication, then, what is needed is a simplified verbal code. This will allow for the team to memorize a limited number of words, which often enables the captain or the stoker to pick the correct word out of the wind noise. Each word can represent a long sentence of instruction, so it is possible to communicate a lot very quickly.

In past conversations with tandem teams, our own verbal code differs from everyone else. Each team will have different issues to address and different things they want or need to be made aware of. Codes also vary depending on the terrain – we have a lot more words for riding off-road than on. At right is our tandem team code. Adapt from it what you need and feel free to make up your own as you gain more insight into what is important for you as a team.

Captain says!

Code	Meaning	On-road	Off-road
Bump	There is a bump coming up that the stoker needs to be made aware of. Not all bumps need to be communicated, but if the bump is likely to jar an unsuspecting stoker, call it out.	✓	✓
Left/ Right	Upcoming direction change. The captain calls this out so the stoker will check behind to verify it is safe to move in that direction.	✓	
Down	The captain is going to shift down to a smaller chainring. Stoker powers back so the shift can happen more easily. As shifting to a smaller chainring results in a more abrupt shifting event (and resulting pedal jerk) than shifting to a smaller cassette cog, I only call out for the former.	✓	✓
Slow	Indicates the captain needs to change through a number of gears by turning the pedals slowly.	✓	✓
Steep	Captain's callout when approaching a steep section of trail. For the stoker, this means to put down more power for a brief period of time and to move back on the seat (increasing traction) as the trail is likely loose.		✓
Easy	Since the stoker cannot see ahead, they may get set into putting down power when it is not wanted. It happens more often than you might think.	✓	✓
Switch	A tight turn is coming up. The stoker should cut power output so the captain can steer the necessary line. Inopportune stoker power can push the tandem straight through a switchback.		✓
Low	A captain's call when a low obstruction is approaching.	✓	✓
'Kay	Captain's reply to indicate acknowledgement of "jacket/water/adjust" from the stoker, or to end the power increase after a "steep" call.	✓	✓
Bell	Captain's request for the stoker to ring the bell. It is easier to make this call than to also have the bell on the captain's bars and take a hand off to ring it while riding.	✓	✓
Pedal up	A call to adjust the pedals for an upcoming sharp turn. If turning left, the left-side pedals should be at the top of the stroke. This is to avoid the pedals striking the pavement.	✓	
Go	Called when a little extra power will help clean a technical feature or switchback.		✓

Stoker says!

Code	Meaning	On-road	Off-road
Clear back	For a "left/right" call by the captain, the stoker will reply with "clear back" if it is safe to turn. These terms are almost exclusively used on the road, when approaching or navigating intersections.	✓	
Up	The stoker needs a higher gear for a more comfortable cadence.	✓	✓
Jacket/ Water/ Adjust	Stoker indicating a need to make an adjustment while on the bike and pedaling. This is an indication to the captain that the ride should remain smooth, so the captain should reply back if the adjustment cannot be accommodated by the conditions.	✓	✓
Ramming speed	A call from the stoker that she wants max speed. This occurs only on flat sections of road or fireroad, requiring top gear and head down.	✓	✓

All play

Code	Meaning	On-road	Off-road
Smooth	This is called out when the partner is mashing the pedals during the crank stroke.	✓	✓
Coast	When one partner needs a break from sitting. This call has the captain set the pedals level and then one or both partners can stand and coast. Stoker always resumes pedaling first when both captain and stoker have reseated.	✓	✓
Stop	Obvious call to stop as soon as possible. Stoker to brace for immediate deceleration. This generally indicates an adjustment that cannot be made while on the bike but can also include getting a bee in your bonnet or other issues that need a stop to resolve.	✓	✓
Pedal	A call to adjust the pedals to the preferred position (flat, left pedal forward). Pedal adjustment is done by the stoker. The captain may call if the pedals are not in the correct starting position, or the stoker may call it out when rotating the pedals, warning the captain to move shins.	✓	✓

During the early days of riding tandem, you will call out a lot more than you need to as you adjust to being a team and figure out exactly what your partner needs to know and when. It is common-sense that teams with years of experience will move from verbal communication to more innate communication. This is especially true if you ride the same roads or trails often; your stoker will remember a route over time and will need fewer calls. Remember, however, that your stoker still cannot see ahead, and trail (or road) conditions change all the time. Just because you have ridden a trail or road route one hundred times before, the captain needs to communicate anything the stoker needs to know.

As a tandem team, we communicate primarily through verbal calls. We do have one physical call, however. If my stoker gooses my waist, that means there is someone coming up behind us, and my stoker does not like to be overtaken. Goosing me means I need to drop a gear and jump on the gas. Why not just come up with a verbal call? We just want to ride off their wheel!

Let's get this party started

If you and your partner are serious about trying this tandem thing, there remain some basics of starting out that are different from starting out on a single bike. The first, of course, is to decide who is up front.

Back in the early days of riding tandem, we had to figure out who was the captain of this ship. (left)

Who's on first?

Generally speaking, tandems are captained by a man. This is not some sexist hold-over from by-gone days, but mostly a matter of physics. While women can run the gears, hit the brakes, and steer as well as men, women cyclists are generally lighter than their partners. This difference in weight (and, extrapolated, to upper body strength) is key to determining tandem roles.

When riding tandem, the stoker spends most of the time seated, especially when stopped for traffic lights or quick breaks. Captains bring the bike to a stop and are responsible for keeping the bike stable and upright. A bike, tandem or no, will fall right over if let go, and this only happens faster when there's a stoker's-worth of

weight way above the tandem's center of gravity. The captain needs to be able to counter the stoker's weight and keep the bike up.

Now, at a stop the captain might have both feet flat on the ground and both hands on the bars, so keeping the bike up is easy. Motorcycle riders have no problems keeping a 500 pound machine up. The tricks begin when you need to start off, at which point you reduce your stability by half once you pick a foot up to put it on the forward pedal. Add in an inopportune stoker movement requiring a counterbalance, and upper-body strength begins to play a bigger role.

It is when you are on the move, however, that strength is most important. Your stoker will reach over for water or to take a jacket off (or put one on) or turn around to look at traffic after a "left" call by the captain. All of these movements, expected and unexpected, need to be countered by the captain to keep the bike upright and pointed in the right direction. The captain needs to do this at mile one and mile 41.

Additionally, some tandems (like our **Burley Duet**) will be more flexy than others (like our rock-solid **El Conquistador de Montañas**). Instead of a small movement when your stoker goes for the water bottle,

13

easily countered on a stiff frame, a flexy frame will require more effort. After a road ride I need to hug my upper arms to stretch and relax them; after an off-road ride, I do not. I am doing much more counterbalancing off-road due to twists, turns, roots, and rocks, but the stiffness of the Ventana frame results in less fatigue.

Beg, borrow, or steal

Before you start worrying about lateral flex, you and your stoker need to spend some quality time on a tandem to see if this is something, in practice, that you both could see yourselves enjoying. There are a couple ways to do this, depending on where you live. And, of course, it should be noted that I did not follow any of the steps in this section. As mentioned in **I had a dream**, we talked about it for a while, then showed up at a bike shop, rode a tandem around the shop, bought it, went home, and took it for our first ride longer than two hundred feet.

Nevertheless, if you live near the coast or a touristy spot, it should be fairly easy to find a bike shop or concessionaire that rents tandems by the hour. Typically these are lower-end, beach-cruiser tandems (see **Tour de beach**) and they will not be that great

and they probably are not maintained to the highest standard. Still, it is a tandem and the flat paths around where these bikes are normally rented can be great places to start out if they are not too crowded.

Alternatively, in this age of the Internet, tandem forums are just a click away. After posting up a request to borrow a tandem for the afternoon, you may find yourself with offers from tandem teams to come and give their bikes a whirl. When we were trying to decide if spending the money on a full-suspension mountain tandem was going to be worth it over the hard-tail off-road tandem we already had (the answer to which is, in every way, yes!), one of the first replies to our question was an offer from a semi-local team to come and try their full-suspension tandem. We ended up buying a local full-suspension tandem shortly after without taking them up on their offer, but during my years of posting on the MTBR.com tandem forum, it was not the only offer made.

Different strokes

One of the most common questions asked of us when we are out on our tandem is, "How is it compared to riding by yourself?" Without taking twenty minutes to go over the basics, the most succinct answer I can give from the front of the bike, pedaling by the questioner, is, "Different!"

Most everything on a tandem is different from riding a single bike, whether on road or off. Some of these differences are better and some are not, and the differences are much greater when riding off-road than on.

When riding off-road, braking is much easier than on a single bike. Due to the length of the bike giving a more stable platform and the riders' positions at the ends of the longer bike, the captain can slam on the brakes in any situation without worrying about locking up the front wheel and flipping over the bars. When climbing steep hills in low gears that would pop up the front wheel of a single bike, a tandem's longer wheelbase and weight over the front ensures the front tire stays planted on the ground.

Whether riding off-road or on, what gravity giveth, gravity taketh away. When riding downhill, you not only enjoy the aero advantage of a tandem (where the stoker is shielded from air resistance but is able to put in 100% power), but gravity is helping you. When climbing, however, there is no aero advantage, gravity is hurting you, and you are essentially a 400 pound rider on a single bike.

I lean, you lean, we lean

Before your first ride, talk to your stoker about leaning. Generally in the tandem world, the captain prefers that the stoker does not lean into turns, similar to riding on the back of a motorcycle. When the captain begins a turn and leans the bike over, a stoker adding lean during the turn will cause the bike to react in ways the captain is not expecting.

We ride so that my stoker remains aligned to the vertical axis of the bike, whether that is perpendicular to the ground or 20° past vertical. I have read stories by off-road teams that employ stoker lean to negotiate tight turns at faster speeds. That is obviously an acquired taste, but the thought of it blows my mind.

In the beginning

Whatever type of tandem you get to try your first ride, it would be best to try it in an open area, preferably one that is paved. This first ride is all about starting, not falling down, and stopping (and not falling down), so the fewer complications the better. An open area or empty backroad will give your stoker a lot more awareness of where you are and where you are going – your stoker will not be able to see ahead, exactly, but will be able to see the road or lot enough to have a general idea and start trusting the pavement will still be there when you get there.

For your first mount, have the captain straddle the bike, with both feet on the ground and both front and rear brakes locked. Whenever my stoker gets on or off the bike, I have my feet on the ground and at least one brake locked. Have the stoker climb on, sit down, and put feet on pedals. You as a team will work out particulars like who adjusts the pedals, when, and how (see **Ten-four good buddy/Pedal**).

Random picture of our tandem taken from inside a burned-out redwood tree trunk. (left)

With your stoker on the bike and the pedals positioned properly, begin riding simply by lifting a foot onto the forward pedal and pushing off like normal. Congratulations, you are riding tandem!

During this initial ride, just concentrate on starting and stopping. When coming to a stop, place one pedal at the bottom of the stroke and stand, apply the brakes, and touch the ground with your other foot. Lock the brakes and quickly place both feet flat on the ground. Then wait for your stoker to adjust the pedals (or call "pedal") and begin again. Once starting and stopping become more natural, start taking long left and right turns, then add shifting gears into the mix. Slowly add complications as you become comfortable. As captain, you brake, turn, and change gears. As a team you put power down and communicate.

One size does not fit all

If your first tandem ride is a rented or borrowed bike, it may not be sized correctly. Most rentable tandems come in one or two sizes, all with the captain's end the same size or larger than the stoker's end. Bike manufacturers assume the captain will be the taller person. As a rented or borrowed bike, it is what it is and you will have to adjust seat height and such as best as you can to accommodate different sizes. If possible, note the size of the tandems you ride so you have something to base a sizing decision if you choose to buy a new or used rig.

When you do start to look for your own tandem, whether mountain or road, pay particular attention to the stoker's cockpit. This is the area of the bike between seatposts. The stoker's cockpit, ideally, will be large enough that you can position the stoker's bars well behind the captain's seat. Stoker stems that hold the stoker's bars are adjustable for height and reach. Provided the stoker's cockpit is long enough for the stoker to sit back, the bars can be adjusted for a comfortable position.

These fitment issues depend specifically on the measurements of each particular tandem team. Most road tandems have a fairly compact stoker cockpit, however, which can put the stoker's bars (and, therefore, hands) right below the captain's seat. If the stoker wants to move hands to the bar's drops, they can contact the captain's legs as he pedals. This is annoying. Similarly, if the stoker's hands are on the flat part of the bars and moves to reposition, there may be some inadvertent hand-to-tush contact. Of course, this is not always inadvertent!

To clip or not to clip, that is the question

Virtually all road and tandem teams I have seen in real life or on the Internet use clipless pedals such as Shimano SPDs. Many people coming from single bikes are used to clipless pedals and transition over without difficulty. I only have a section on this subject because I, personally, do not use clipless pedals on our tandems. I use platform pedals. My stoker uses platforms off-road and clipless pedals on-road.

This is mostly a product of never having used clipless setups on my single bikes. Growing up I had BMX bikes through college, so I was fairly stuck in my ways (nevermind extremely used to not being clipped in) by the time I got my first mountain bike. Since pulling on the upstroke was something I had never done before, I stuck with what I knew.

If you are experienced with clipless pedals on your other bikes, it makes sense to start tandeming with the same pedal setup. Platform pedals can help with stoker trepidation, however. I have also found that a quick dab can keep you upright off-road, and I much prefer the stability of two rubber-soled feet on the ground at stop lights on the road. Your experience will vary, but I put this in here to suggest that platform pedals can be an option, even if it is not common in cycling or tandem circles.

The captain has turned on the "No Stopping!" sign

I am the captain of a tandem and my jobs are many. Primarily, they boil down to two main goals: Keeping the bike **Rubber-side down**; keeping my stoker happy. Occasionally those goals cannot both be met at the same time, in which case my only goal is to keep the bike **Rubber-side down**.

Rubber-side down

On the road, keeping the tandem on two wheels should present no issues. Which is not to say we have never gone down on the road. You may have noticed an interesting choice of words in that last sentence. While it is Job #1 for the captain to keep the bike upright, if and when you do crash, you both go down. See **Rubber-side up** for more thoughts on this uniquely tandem experience.

As mentioned above, road riding should present few issues that threaten the bike or the team. Road obstacles are typically easy to see with warning, there tends to be more room in which to avoid, intersections are open and controlled by signs or signals. As captain, you still have to maintain a high level of alertness as cars, people, and dogs (or even squirrels) do come out of the darnedest places. Road riding brings much higher speeds (both peak and average) over the course of a ride and any problem becomes a bigger problem at higher speed.

When taking your tandem off-road, most of the road-riding issues are removed (except those pesky squirrels!). In their place are substituted a list of new issues, including:

- Oncoming riders on singletrack trails with short visibility windows (read: tight turns amongst tall flora).

- Variable trail conditions, even from one ride to the next on the same trails.

- Certain sun angles creating difficulty reading the trail.

- Water crossings with unknown obstacles (rocks, branches, etc.).
- Tight turns, rocks, and exposure all on the same bit of trail.

We have logged thousands of miles riding tandem on the road with only one notable "off." We have logged thousand of miles of riding tandem off-road with more than one notable "off." Our higher crash rate off-road is mainly attributable to the variability of trail conditions and my failure to properly read the trail bed. **Rubber-side up** will dissect the lessons learned from some of our lower moments.

In captain I trust

In keeping the **Rubber-side down** you are achieving your main goal as a captain of a tandem. Only slightly less important is to maintain the trust of your stoker. This was discussed more fully in **T R U S T, tell you what it means to me**, but that was more from what the stoker expects and requires. What is that issue like from the front seat?

Approaching a steep, rocky section of trail in Cheeseboro National Recreation Area. Here I have called out "coast" and "bump" so that I can get the pedals level and we can both stand to absorb the rock hits. (left) Photo credit: Jim Henderson.

As captain, you basically need to avoid spooking your stoker. With no control and limited sight ahead, this is no small task. With proper line choice, communication, and awareness of the abilities and desires of your stoker, it really should be second nature to gain and maintain your stoker's trust.

Proper line choice on the road can include maintaining a safe distance from parked and moving cars and choosing routes that offer at least a modicum of bike lane. Extremely vehicle-dense roads are not fun to ride on single bikes and they are not any more fun to ride tandem. One way to mitigate (but by no means eliminate) traffic concerns is to fit rear-view mirrors. Fitted to road bikes these are typically attached to the outsides of the handlebars, but versions can also be mounted on helmets. This view behind you gives more awareness of passing traffic so you can prepare as necessary.

Stoker's rear-view mirror on our Burley. Cheap and functional.

Proper line choice off-road focuses even more on your stoker's abilities and desires. Exposure, a large drop just off the side of a trail, can be the biggest issue for your stoker. While you know exactly where the trail is going, your stoker cannot see ahead but has full view of that large drop just off the side. Running the bike toward the inside of the trail, furthest from the exposure, and communicating the trail ahead at this time will go a long way. Planning ahead also helps with any other trail;

picking a route freer of big rocks is much appreciated by your stoker.

Communication, beyond the code words described in **Ten-four good buddy**, helps build stoker confidence immensely. If your stoker can visualize the upcoming road/terrain, they know what to prepare for. In the first weeks and months of riding tandem, your communication to your stoker, and vice-versa, will be much more frequent than years down the road.

Due to riding many of the same trails week in and week out, my verbal communication to my stoker has diminished considerably. Not only is she familiar enough with the trails to know what is coming and when, she is also very aware of what I need from her with respect to certain trail and road intersections we transit on every ride. When we ride in new areas, our communication increases a bit over normal, but our speed will also have dropped a bit over normal to keep the **Rubber-side down** and trust up.

Awareness of stoker ability includes sticking to roads and trails your stoker is comfortable with and changing ride qualities (speed, gear, distance) to accommodate your stoker's needs. That sentence encompasses a huge amount of compromise, but that is the underlying facet of riding tandem. And that is not to say you can never push your stoker onto a new trail or for a longer ride – growing in trust will bring about growth in ability and a desire for new rides.

Trust is a two-way street

As mentioned in **Set up for success**, trust flows both ways, and as captain you need to have trust in your stoker as well. While your stoker does not have controls, per-se, a stoker certainly will be able to influence the bike and your ride. Stokers should follow all verbal codes (see **Ten-four good buddy**) appropriately. As a captain, I will not call out "slow" unless I need to change through a number of gears in preparation, typically, for an imminent climb or obstacle. If I need to change a lot of gears I need my stoker to ease up on her power so that the changes can be made quickly and cleanly.

On the road, if you call out "left," you need your stoker to check behind to see if a left turn is safe to make. As captain, you are already multitasking steering the bike and scanning the road ahead. Not only does your stoker need to check traffic behind quickly, there needs to be immediate reciprocal communication back to you that the turn is safe to make, "clear back," or not safe to make, "no!" This is a stoker responsibility.

Additionally, stokers need to communicate with the captain as concisely as possible. If the stoker needs another gear or some other accommodation, captains are only too happy to change gear, etc., but timing is everything. If a stoker tries to communicate the need for a higher gear because of how spinning makes an old knee injury come back and cause pain…well, that is way more information than we need up front. Similarly, a stoker request may be quashed simply due to changing conditions or terrain. A stoker may call for a gear change, but if as captain you see ahead that the request will put you into the wrong gear for the upcoming conditions (or whatever the issue may be), the captain must veto.

Attention on deck

Tandems attract attention from cyclists and pedestrians alike. Cycling is still a niche activity and riding tandem is a niche-iest of niches. When we ride off-road on the trails near us, where we have ridden tandem for 10 years, we still get people telling us they have never seen an off-road tandem.

Get used to attention. Luckily, almost all that attention is positive. People love tandems. Maybe they love the idea of riding tandem, or maybe they are just attracted to the rarity of seeing something new.

It ain't easy being green

Unfortunately, a number of people (whether on bikes themselves, or on foot) feel the need to trump out some version of the tired tattle, "She's not pedaling!" Mainly this is spoken by people as a joke, but I personally feel that some of those people (and all of the rest who do not indicate it as a joke) are just jealous. Here we are, working as a team to get up a hill, down a drop, enjoying each other's company out on the roads or trails of coastal California, and someone comes to try to throw a damp rag on it.

Truth be told, I just roll my eyes, maybe I give a snort, and keep on truckin'. My stoker, however, takes great umbrage at those sorts of comments, and for damn good reason. Again, I view it as expressions of jealousy. When men say it, they are jealous they are not out with their partners. When women say it, they are jealous they are not out with their partners. Nevertheless, the comment is directed at my stoker and she does not appreciate it.

When we are stopped for a break and someone asks a version of, "Can you feel it if she stops pedaling?," which is the same basic tattle rephrased, I can only reply that if my stoker were not pedaling, we would be going nowhere. Yes, I can certainly feel if she is not pedaling (or putting in too much power) through the timing chain. Trust me, I know. Again, this is often piqued curiosity at seeing something people may rarely see, but from the stoker's point of view it is some degree of insulting.

All dressed up

As a tandem team, you can moderate the attention somewhat depending on your riding attire. Choose different colors for captain and stoker and you decrease the attention you draw. Conversely, if you pick matching jerseys that day, and particularly if your matching jerseys prominently feature, say, Spanky, the maniacal cymbal-smashing monkey, expect more people to look your way and say something.

Speaking of our Spanky jerseys, you will have noticed that most pictures in this book have us in those self-same jerseys. Though we have other bike jerseys, and other matching bike jerseys, our Spanky jerseys are a part of our tandem riding. My stoker bought them as a wedding present to me (which I did not know was a thing). If we have back-to-back riding days we will obviously be in a different jersey one of those days, but if the question is between a freshly-laundered Spanky and any other jersey, Spanky gets the nod!

Monkeying around in Monterey. (right)

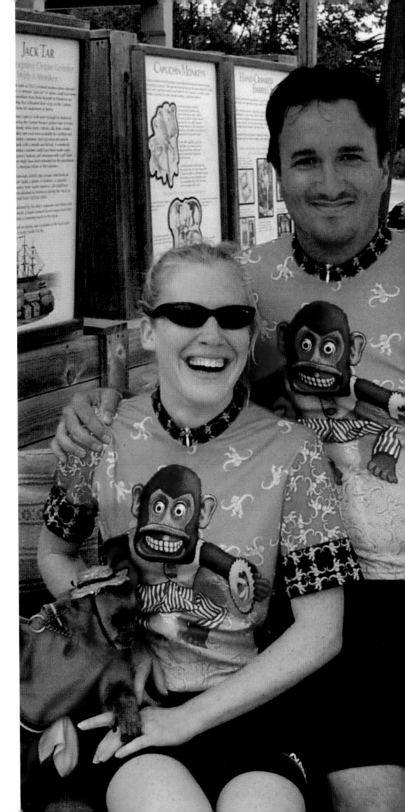

Tandemachina

For being a niche of a niche, tandem bicycles come in many flavors and are more popular than ever. Before I get into describing the various types of tandem, there are a couple tandem-specific bike terms to define.

The vast majority of parts on a tandem are the same as those on a single bike of the same type (road or mountain). The only parts that differ are those between the seats:

- Boom tube – the bottom frame tube between the captain and stoker cranksets.
- Timing chain (aka sync chain) – the longer of the two chains on a tandem, linking the captain and stoker cranks together.
- Captain's cranks – the forward set of cranks which are typically left-hand-drive and connect the timing chain to the stoker's cranks.
- Stoker's cockpit – includes the area between the seats, specifically the stoker's handlebars and stem, and the frame's top tube between seat posts.

Tour de beach

In certain areas of the country, a very common tandem is the beach cruiser tandem, also known as the tourist rental tandem. As mentioned in **Beg, borrow, or steal**, finding one of these to rent for an afternoon is a cheap way to see if tandeming might be something you and your partner enjoy. The experience will be somewhat-to-significantly different than borrowing a high-end road or mountain tandem, but as a way to dip your toes, it can work well.

Beach cruiser-style tandems are the easiest to transition to from single bike riding. Beach cruiser tandems have more upright positioning for the riders, which affords the stoker the clearest view ahead. Cruiser tandems are built with fairly low bottom-bracket heights (a standard frame measurement of the distance between the ground and the center of the crankset axle), which means easier mounting, dismounting, and often the ability to put feet on the ground while sitting on the seat. These features are very useful to overcome stability concerns.

Rental tandems are, for the most part, a lot like rental cars — they are base-model strippers without bells or whistles, may not have been ridden with all that much care, and probably have not been maintained to a high standard. This is stated just to make you aware that if you have issues with the bike during your first tandem ride, it probably is just an issue with the bike and not with you as a team.

A great example of the beach cruiser-style tandem is the Schwinn Tango. Schwinn brought out their beach-cruiser tandem in the mid-2000s and I was drawn to it immediately. Reasonably priced at its debut at $600, if I had space in the garage to store yet another tandem, it would have been ours. It is a perfect tandem for riding around town and, yes, cruising along the beach.

Virtually all of the cruiser-style tandems are on the lower-end of component specification. With complete tandems available from Schwinn for approximately $800 today (2016), they represent perhaps the highest specification available, but still feature components (namely wheels and drivetrain) that may not stand the test of a heavy or aggressive team. As fat tandems become more popular, high-end cruiser builds will probably migrate towards their all-terrain cousins.

Tour de road

Away from the beach, and particularly on the East Coast, the tandem road bike is easily the most common tandem with the largest number of manufacturers and build options. Any technology currently featured on single road bikes has already made its way to road tandems, including electronic shifting and a wide selection of material choice (steel, aluminum, carbon fiber, titanium, bamboo, etc.).

Road tandems are the most popular tandem in large part because road riding is the type of riding most people are familiar with and have access to. The transition from single road bikes to riding tandem is fairly easy, though because of the increased speeds and more aggressive rider positioning, there may be a higher bar for stokers new to riding to overcome when climbing on the back.

On road tandems, stokers are generally tucked up fairly close behind their captains. This is great for aerodynamics and for the business of blasting through the miles of your route. This is not so great for stoker forward vision – of the three main types of tandems (cruiser, road, mountain), road tandems most restrict stoker vision ahead.

Additionally, a stoker's room to move and adjust may also be reduced, also due to typical road tandem geometry. In **One size does not fit all** I talk about a couple issues that result, particularly limited hand positions for my stoker during a ride. Due also to the more aggressive positioning, I cannot wear my CamelBak as it occupies space my stoker would prefer for her face.

One key component all road tandems should have is a quality suspension seatpost for the stoker position. This is not negotiable, and if your new-to-you road tandem does not have a good suspension seatpost for your stoker, please install one before the first ride. Road bikes, tandem or single, run small-volume tires at high pressures, so there is no forgiveness to the ride quality over broken or pocked pavement. When on a single bike, you can react quickly (by standing or unweighting the bike), but you are not unweighting a tandem, and standing must be a coordinated effort communicated to, and understood by, your stoker…by which time you have likely already hit whatever pothole was in the way.

A quality suspension seatpost will allow stokers to remain seated, and pedaling, while smoothing out most of the road noise. Quality suspension posts generally start with names like Thudbuster and not names like Nashbar. The cost difference is reflected in stoker ratings, and a happy stoker is key to tandeming.

Burley Duet

My then-girlfriend and I were both riders and had talked about tandeming for the last few months, but we did not follow my own advice in this book by going down to the beach and renting a cruiser tandem for the day. Instead, in 2003 my girlfriend of one year accompanied me to our local bike store. They had a sale tag on last year's Burley Duet. After a spin around the store, we took it home and began trying to figure out how to make it all work. And where to park it!

Burley Duet, our road tandem and our first jump into riding together. Love it to bits, wish it were slightly bigger.

Burley, at the time, was an employee-owned co-op located in Oregon. Their road tandems were solid bikes with good components, and the Duet tandem made up a large portion of their bike output based on used bikes I have seen for sale. For the vast majority of its life, our Duet retained all of its original components, aside from wear items like tires, the aforementioned suspension seatpost replacement, and the addition of a drag brake. It was only upgraded to 10-speed with the demise of its right/rear shift lever. This is a testament to the original component selection, and the easy miles covered over the road.

My main issue with our Duet concerned frame flex. The Duet was constructed of steel tubes, where the most common tandem frame material is stiffer aluminum. That said, our Ventana El Conquistador de Montañas S&S (see **New Bigfoot rising**) and our **Co-Motion Java** are constructed of steel tubes as well and exhibit no flex. The Duet's flex was caused by stoker movement (reaching for water, turning to check on traffic) twisting the frame. As captain, I needed to compensate for this twisting before the bike's new momentum sends us off our line. Any ride on the Duet was a continuous, but mostly unconscious, battle with frame flex. This resulted mainly in sore upper arms, but it impacted how long we could ride per day.

Our Duet was built with V brakes, a style more popular on mountain bikes (before disc brakes came out) and while they stopped the tandem just fine, the speeds we were attaining in our early days on the downhills were starting to spook the stoker **and** the captain. Dragging a rim brake (applying some braking force over a long period of time) to attenuate speed downhill was not really an option. Dragging rim brakes builds heat into the rims, tubes, and tires, and this can result in a tube or tire failure at speed.

The solution was the installation of an Arai drag brake (see **What a drag**). Essentially a cable-operated drum brake, the drag brake threaded on to the rear hub opposite the cassette. Burley had outfitted their tandems with not only a rear hub threaded for the drag brake, but also a tab mounted on the frame to bolt the drag brake's arm. Installation could not have been easier thanks to this forward thinking. After installation, when we would descend and want to limit speed, I engaged the drag brake, leaving both hands and both rim brakes free.

We put thousands of miles on our Duet, but our introduction to tandeming off-road (see **Ventana El Conquistador de Montañas**) began a serious reduction in road trips. On most bike paths and routes locally (such as the **Ventura River Trail**, or VRT), I grew to prefer larger-volume tires to absorb road vibration. I spent the decade-plus of Burley ownership moving to larger tires, from the original 700c25, to 700c28, to 700c32, and finally to 700c35 cyclocross tires. Those 35s were the largest tires that would fit the frame, but they just were not enough.

Our Burley with 700c35 cyclocross tires. I was slowly turning our road bike into an off-road bike, but I got soft after buying our Ventana. And after getting older.

Each upsize improved the ride at a small cost of efficiency, but it was nowhere near the plushness (and vastly decreased pedaling efficiency) of our Ventana. We have taken our mountain tandem on the Monterey Bay Coastal Trail (a paved, separated bike path) and VRT, but the upright body positioning was good for only about 20 miles - any more and we were sore. We needed a Plan B.

Tour de gravel

The newest niche within the niche that is tandem cycling is the adventure tandem, better known as the gravel grinder. Gravel grinders are the current hot topic in the single road world, where riders have come over to my way of thinking, espoused in my quest for bigger tires on the **Burley Duet** - bigger is better.

Gravel grinders are, more or less, road bikes built to take 40-55mm tires, or up to a 2.1" width in old money. These bikes also have disc brakes exclusively, though most any serious road tandem will be disc-based at this point. Gravel grinders will also tend to have maximum accessory mounting points for things like multiple water bottle cages, fenders, racks front and rear, etc.

I first cottoned on to the idea of a gravel-grinder tandem by seeing a post on MTBTandem's Facebook page. They had converted one of their Fandango hardtail mountain tandem frames (welded by Ventana, see **Ventana El Conquistador de Montañas**) to drop-bars, the typical handlebars used for road bikes, and the requisite road brifters and drivetrain.

That post immediately answered the question of how to make our Burley more comfortable on the road - by replacing it entirely with a new tandem! Coincidentally, it also answered the question of how make the Burley have a longer stoker cockpit - by replacing it entirely with a new tandem, of course!

To that point, we had not thought about buying a new road tandem. We had a perfectly serviceable road tandem in the Burley, and we had no idea they made drop-bar tandems (nee: road) that would take big tires. However, upon learning of the possibility, it fairly quickly progressed to looking at options.

As a niche within a niche, the selection is pretty slim as of the update to this book (2018). There is the aforementioned Fandango sold at MTBTandems. This had price going for it (complete bikes from the low $4,000 range, depending on parts specification), and quality given it is manufactured by the group at Ventana.

Other high-end road tandem manufactures like Santana do not offer anything in the gravel-grinder category. Calfee can build you something to accommodate your wide-tire needs, however Calfee was out of our price range given their carbon fiber construction pushing frame-only costs that start ~$8,000.

Mainstream manufactures like Cannondale offer rigid tandems with room for wide tires, however they build these bikes with mountain-style flat bars, geometry, and gearing. Having ridden our Ventana mountain tandem on a 40-mile road ride, there is more to a comfortable long-distance road bike than just converting to drop bars. Companies like Trek are not in the game at all.

The selection was narrowed further because, well, if we were going to buy a new tandem to fix the first problem of fitting wider tires, we should also fix the second problem of the stoker compartment. The Burley's stoker cockpit (measured center-to-center between the seat posts or at the crank centers) was 26.8". The Fandango offered up 28.5" of stoker cockpit; 28.5" seemed to be the current standard for road tandems across a number of manufacturers. The problem was, we were not sure it was enough.

As happens in the bike world, and particularly seems to happen in the tandem world (see **New Bigfoot rising**), at least to us, mission creep set in. IF we were going to buy a new tandem so we could run wider tires on the road, and IF it also made a sort of sense to buy a new tandem so we could get a bike with a longer stoker cockpit, then why would we not spend a little bit extra and get what we really wanted? 28.5" as standard was only 1.7" longer than the Burley, and would 1.7" really add enough to make my stoker comfortable, especially given the cost? Perhaps, and we tried to mock it up on the Duet, but then the observation was made that even if the 1.7" additional was enough for comfort, it definitely was not enough to provide room for me to wear my pack.

When we ride the Ventana, I wear a CamelBak that holds sunscreen, a light First Aid kit, and a wealth of bike supplies like tubes, tools, cables, and other small parts that would get us out of a jam in the backcountry. There had never been room to wear it on the Burley (see **Tour de road**), and while we mostly did not needed anything the pack contained, we did pass roadies from time to time who were at the side of the road attempting repair. I never bothered to stop because I had no tools or supplies to offer them.

If we had never really used the supplies in the pack, why was this now a potential issue? The purchase of a gravel grinder would open up some ride variations that would see us in the backcountry (see **Newbury Park Surf Loop**), places (and surfaces) we would not attempt on the Burley. Besides, for companies that offer customized geometry, the typical charge for this is a few hundred dollars. To go all the way to buying a new multi thousand-dollar tandem only to gain 1.7" when, for a few dollars more, we could gain, say, another 2" on top of that, well...there is some sense there, I think you will agree.

But wait, there is more mission creep! As mentioned earlier in this section, having ridden our Ventana on a long road ride and found it wanting for comfort towards the end, we began to think about adding S&S couplers (see **Coupling couplers**) to this new tandem purchase. There is a long-dreamed-but-not-planned vacation taking our tandem to Germany and touring the country. However, if it was not going to be ideal in the likely conditions of road/path riding between small German towns, maybe adding couplers to the gravel grinder would be a smart move?

We were now looking for a gravel grinder, we were looking for custom geometry, and we were looking for couplers. Where did that leave us? We thought one shop could accommodate our dreams and our wallet - Co-Motion Cycles.

Co-Motion Java

Co-Motion is an established name in the adventure biking world. They produce a wide range of single bikes suited for cross-country or cross-world cycling. Co-Motion also has a range of road tandems and has recently refined their gravel-grinder options.

Co-Motion offers two tandems in the gravel-grinder category, the Mocha running 27.5"/650b wheels and the Java with 29"/700c wheels. For a road-based bike, the bigger wheels are the way to go, if not for reasons of pedalling efficiency then for reasons of tire selection - there are more and cheaper 29" tires out there. The standard Java will take approximately a 2.1" tire, and Co-Motion has an available "2.5 yoke" for the rear that provides all the room you need.

The stock rear 1.9" tire paired with the 2.5 yoke option. Lots of room for growth.

Co-Motion charges $495 for custom geometry. What does that get you for your money? It gets you a conversation with their frame designer, a custom frame drawing, and the resulting frame that requires one-off tubing and jig to build. As mentioned in **Tour de gravel**, the custom charge is a small price to pay for an extra 2" of stoker cockpit.

If you are also ordering the frame built with S&S couplers, one major consideration during your custom frame discussion is to ensure the resulting frame will fit into the cases. We have S&S hardcases, which have very fixed dimensions. Co-Motion sells their own softcases, where dimensions are slightly more malleable. Co-Motion will need to keep the hardcase dimensional limitations in mind when designing your frame, as coupler placement along the tubes impacts how the frame breaks down to fit in the cases. See **Order up** for our ordering experience.

Co-Motion Java Co-Pilot ready to hit the road. Big tires, and nearly 4" of additional stoker cockpit! (above).

Co-Motion charges $1600 for S&S couplers on their tandem frames. This is the price only for the couplers, as cases, wrenches, grease, and padding are all optional extras. By comparison, Ventana up-charges roughly the same amount for a coupled tandem frame, however with Ventana you get all of the above included in the price (cases retail for $500 each) **and** a fifth coupler. Ventana builds their tandem frames with a "lateral" tube, the tube that runs diagonally from the head tube down to the stoker's bottom bracket. However, Ventana was not interested in building us a gravel grinder. I asked.

Our new gravel grinder, named Fred, was ordered to give us vastly more comfort on the road due to larger tires and longer stoker cockpit. It offered a longer-distance riding option when traveling. And it opened up some new part road/part dirt rides we could do from our door.

Tour de mountain

Mountain tandems – tandems build specifically for off-road conditions – are the rarest of the three main types of tandem (cruiser, road, mountain). In any given area it is uncommon to see one. Despite the number of road tandem rallies (long-weekend riding events), there remains only one organized off-road tandem rally, the semi-regular Appalachian Off-Road Tandem Adventure (AORTA). To be fair, the vast majority of road-tandem rallies have also been on the East Coast, which seems (for no reason I can think of) to be a relative hot-bed of tandems and tandemists. We are a bit jealous here on the West Coast.

Amongst the redwood forests of Samuel P. Taylor State Park in California. (right)

So you are unlikely to see a mountain tandem in the wild. As with beach cruiser-style tandems and road tandems, a mountain tandem is basically just a single mountain bike with a stoker's cockpit between the captain's seat and the rear wheel. Mountain tandems are as up-to-date as their road-tandem cousins, featuring the latest technologies and materials.

Road tandems are substantially similar across manufacturers because they are built to perform in substantially similar conditions, that of riding on pavement. Mountain tandems, however, in the last few years have flowered into a wide variety of solutions for a wide variety of conditions. Your choices when looking at mountain tandems include:

- Wheel size, from old-school 26", to 29ers, to 27.5", to + sizes of each of those, all the way to fat-bikes.

- Suspension type, from no suspension front or rear (known as a rigid bike), to front suspension, but no rear (known as a hard-tail), to suspension at the front and back (known as full-suspension).

With these options, you can create the perfect mountain tandem for your conditions (see **Buy high, sell low**). While there are very few conditions in which you would really want a rigid mountain tandem, the choices in suspension and tire size mean you can build a plush all-mountain rig or a lighter, focused race bike. Or one that works great in snow (or sand)! When looking at new and used bikes, keep in mind that some rigid bikes (see **KHS Tandemania**) can be converted into hard-

tails by adding a suspension fork, and they can be a less-expensive way to get off road together.

KHS Tandemania

A few years after beginning our road tandem adventure together, my stoker and I started thinking about tandeming off the beaten path. At this time we both had single mountain bikes and had already started to shift our riding time to the mountains. While we immediately started dreaming of full-suspension tandem goodness, the associated price tag of many thousands of dollars required we find a way to convince ourselves the money would be well-spent.

At this point we did not even know if we wanted to ride tandem off-road. We had ridden our **Burley Duet** off-road once when the captain (me) did not want to face 10 miles of headwinds, instead taking a canyon fireroad shortcut through **Point Mugu State Park** to get home. This involved seven miles of fireroad on a road tandem with road tires and very little ground clearance. It was at the same time garbage (speeds were mostly single-digit miles per hour, it was incredibly bumpy) and eye-opening (maybe we could ride trails together).

Our KHS Tandemania, after some upgrades to add front suspension and better braking, etc. (right)

I started looking at low-end mountain tandems as a way to explore this new scene. KHS' Tandemania was their road tandem fitted with flat mountain-bike handlebars instead of dropped road handlebars, and it was a compromised bike as a result:

- It was a rigid bike
- It had road-based frame geometry
- It had road-based gearing (53 tooth big ring!)
- It had unsuitable brakes for riding off-road
- It had much larger timing chain rings that further reduced ground clearance

On the plus side, our local Craigslist had a post offering a nearly-new Tandemania for $600. As detailed in **Buy high, sell low**, there are really only two kinds of used tandems that you can buy, the break-up sale or the upgrade sale. The KHS was a break-up sale in that half of the tandem team had no intention of ever getting on the bike again. So with approximately 50 miles on the bike, we picked it up for 60% off retail.

While we did tool around town on it after bringing it home, its debut on the dirt had to wait for some upgrades. The rigid front fork was changed out for a suspension fork with disc brake mounts. This upgrade, coupled with a Brake Therapy rear disc adapter, allowed us to mount disc brakes, replacing the factory V brakes. Wider riser handlebars were added front and back. Finally the original rigid stoker's seat post was changed out for a suspension post.

With these modifications, the KHS was an adequate off-road machine. We had regular shifting issues due to our local bike shop having difficulty tuning road-bike derailleurs to work with flat-bar shifters (all original KHS equipment). The gearing, also original KHS, was not optimal for steep dirt trails, though the 53-tooth big ring up front was great for bombing down fireroads.

After a few months, however, the biggest issue with the KHS was brought to prominence. We were getting bored with fireroads and, as our confidence grew on dirt, we started to leave them for twisty singletrack. Singletrack that was more bumpy than the fireroads. Combining the speed with the bumps proved a rough ride for my stoker, even with the suspension post.

We only spent a few months with our KHS. We loved riding tandem off road and needed a bike that was more capable. At right is a preview of what is coming next, shown here on Los Robles trail in Thousand Oaks, CA. (right)

As there was still speed to be had if my stoker could hang on, we again started dreaming of full-suspension goodness. Only now we knew we loved riding tandem off-road even more than we did on it. At this point we had not made a conscious decision to buy a full-suspension tandem, but we had just bought a house in large part because it was near the off-road trails we were gravitating to.

And then a break-up sale full-suspension tandem, in the right size, popped up in our very city just a few weeks later that was better equipped than we would have been able to afford new. Well, that is just serendipity throwing us a big ol' bone.

Ventana El Conquistador de Montañas

While we knew we could not afford a brand new full-suspension tandem, our relationship with Ventana actually started before the purchase of our El Conquistador de Montañas (ECdM, for short) off Craigslist. I had kept my eye on eBay auctions to get an idea of prices, specification, and just general availability of used tandems, and a Ventana ECdM frame popped up for $1000, but in an 18/14 size. While I was at work the next day, my wife called Ventana to see if they could tell us if this frame size might fit our particular measurements.

When I returned home from work, my wife told me about her conversation, and that after discussing her problem with the woman who answered the phone, she was put on with a guy named "Sherwood" who talked to her for fifteen minutes about the used frame and fitment. The guy suggested that it might fit and that even if it did not, the trade-in value with Ventana was worth more than the auction price, so we could not lose. Once her story was finished, I told my wife that Sherwood (Gibson) was the owner of the company, whom she had chatted up about buying a used frame and received only encouragement. This was a company we could get behind.

> Riding all around Bend, Oregon, on our new ECdM. We stopped long enough to set up this shot, but immediately had to get moving again to try to avoid mosquitoes. That did not work, completely... (right)

A few weeks later, a co-worker of mine sent me a Craigslist link to the Ventana ECdM we bought the next day. As mentioned at the end of **KHS Tandemania**, it was in our preferred 17/16 size and was just down the street from my work. The bike sold itself, with a

specification above that which we would have allowed ourselves to purchase new, but the *coup de grace* was the test ride. We had not even adjusted the seats and handlebars, and the pedals were clipless where we were wearing tennis shoes, and we were looking at the bike in city and not on the trail.

I rode the bike straight off the curb...and my stoker shouted, "SOLD!"

We were the proud owners of a mint, well-spec'ed full-suspension tandem, paying 50% of new. We called it Bigfoot since our ECdM was metallic blue (sorry, Cosmic Blue) and had huge tires, just like the original monster truck. Unfortunately a few days later my stoker went in for knee surgery and we could not ride our new tandem for six months. Dark days, indeed.

Our new-to-us off-road tandem lived up to our expectations, and then some. For more than a year of riding we tried to catch up to the capabilities of the bike:

- The enhanced rigidity was a leap beyond the KHS (which itself was much stiffer than our **Burley Duet**), reducing captain fatigue and

helping me stick to the line I wanted, instead of the line the KHS might instead have picked.

- The extended stoker cockpit allowed for independent placement of the captain's seat and stoker's handlebars. No longer were my stoker's differing hand positions during a ride affecting me in any way. This was also beneficial for my stoker, as she had free choice of hand positions.

- The frame, specifically the rear triangle, was built to accept wide, high-volume tires. The largest tire I could fit on the KHS was a 26x2.2", where I run 26x2.5" tires on Bigfoot. That 0.3" might seem insignificant, but the actual tires on the bike are of dramatically different sizes.

- Finally, the rear suspension was a godsend. There was an immediate, massive improvement in ride comfort for my stoker, which allowed for longer rides. The rear suspension allowed us greater speeds on trails. It also allowed me to take different lines on our usual trails and opened up new trails to us that were not comfortable or possible on the KHS.

Bigfoot down

As Bigfoot approaches 10 years with us, I have to acknowledge that we are not riding the original used frame we bought in 2007. In 2011 after a mountain bike trip to Bend, Oregon, I was doing a routine tear-down of the bike when I noticed a crack in the metallic blue powder coat.

The crack, an unwelcome development.

Powder coat does not really crack (it chips, it can be scuffed, sure), so fearing the worst I wire-wheeled the powder coat off in that area and…exposed the crack in the underlying metal. I took a picture and e-mailed Ventana. Later that afternoon I received an e-mail back from Ventana. For $500 they could fix our frame by cutting out the broken part and welding in a new piece. In the process, since they would have to strip the powder coat off to weld, the repair fee included a complete powder coat and new stickers.

For those thinking that the above is somewhat of a raw deal, Ventana does not offer a lifetime warranty. We were also not the original owners of the frame. Lastly, companies that do offer a lifetime warranty will not repair **your** frame, they only give you a then-current frame as a replacement. Whether the current component standards are the same as your original frame (in other words, if all the parts from your old frame fit the new frame) is your problem. In our case, Ventana was going to fix **our** frame and return it to us. One week, door-to-door, our frame returned, in a blazing coat of Ferrari Red. What happened to Cosmic Blue? When talking with Ventana about the repair, they asked us what color we wanted.

In an ideal world, I would prefer to have our own frame repaired and have that repair covered under a lifetime warranty. Of the two real-world options outlined above, I actually prefer Ventana's way. I like that our bike can be fixed (and not junked), that I could deal directly with the manufacturer, that the turn-around was a week (we went from riding to disassembly to riding within two weekends), and that we got to pick a new color.

Our refurbished ECdM in Ferrari Red. Lovely.

But with the refurbished frame back from Ventana, was this not the perfect time to sell it off and upgrade?

New Bigfoot rising

It was. I was able to sell off our refurbished frame and separately take advantage of Ventana's trade-in program to get a fairly large discount off the price of a new frame. My wife and I have future hopes of traveling and would love to hit some sweet foreign singletrack. What if we could do that with our own tandem? One of Ventana's endless options is a frame built with S&S couplers, which allows the bike to be disassembled and fitted into two airline-approved cases, enabling us to travel the world with Bigfoot (see **Coupling couplers**).

Interestingly, Ventana makes their S&S frames from steel instead of their normal material of choice: aluminum. I was initially wary of steel as a tandem frame material due to my experience with the **Burley Duet**. Since I was dealing with Ventana, I just called and spoke with Sherwood, the owner. As you do. We had a 15 minute conversation where he convinced me I would not notice any additional flex from the steel frame. And after putting the new frame on the same trails we knew well on our original ECdM, he was absolutely correct.

Since we were going to be up in the area when our new S&S ECdM was ready to ship, we arranged to pick it up at Ventana instead. Even this sounds pretty abnormal – how many people will go to the Giant factory in Taiwan to pick up their new frame? – but it gets even better. We were driving up on a Saturday, yet Ventana's business manager volunteered to come to the shop and open the doors for us on her day off. Not only that, but once there she gave us a shop tour! Talk about nirvana. And talk about customer service!

Our Ventana El Conquistador de Montanas S&S, fresh from the factory.

The S&S couplers that make our ECdM even more special. (right)

Buy high, sell low

Having read this far into the book, you and your partner are keen to start looking for your new tandem. You could do it the way we bought our first tandem – show up at a bike shop and check out what they have on the floor. Or you could read a little further while I talk about all the things I have learned since buying the **Burley Duet**.

If the bike does not fit, you must acquit

Whether the tandem in question is a good deal or a screaming deal, if the bike does not fit you and your partner correctly, it will be money wasted. Finding a tandem that is comfortable for you **both** is key.

Some tandem manufacturers like Ventana, Calfee, or Co-Motion among others, are experts on their bikes and will have a conversation directly with you about their bikes, sizes offered, and which might be the best choice for you and your partner given your measurements. Those tandem manufacturers, and others like Co-Motion, will also build frames with custom geometry.

Larger bike companies and conglomerates that do not focus on tandems, such as Trek or Cannondale, will refer you to their dealer network, where it is very much a take-it-or-leave-it proposition. As tandems are relatively rare, many dealers are unlikely to be experts when it comes to tandems. The Internet can help you find dealers with tandem knowledge, but those stores may not be located in your neighborhood.

I harp on tandem size in large part because our **Burley Duet** was not the perfect fit. As we bought a tandem with little knowledge and no comparison shopping, the fact that we could fit on the bike did not mean it was the correct size. Burley at the time had only three frame sizes to choose and the bike shop only had one tandem on the floor. Of the three sizes Burley offered, our Duet was the size closest to what we needed, but it still was not right. Many hours were spent adjusting seats, heights, stems, and bars, but we still had to compensate for the undersized frame. The main fit issue was the cramped stoker cockpit. This had always been an issue for us specifically (in no small part because my stoker is closer in height and reach to me, which is not the case for all teams), but it was put into stark relief upon buying our **Ventana El Conquistador de Montañas**.

The most important thing you can do with a tandem you are looking to buy is to ride it before purchase. If buying new, ask about the different sizes offered and work with the bike shop making adjustments. A tandem has to be comfortable for you, your stoker, and you as a team, so this is not something you can hop on, ride around the shop, then take home. Trust me.

Used tandem superstore

What are the advantages of buying a used tandem? Bicycles in general do not hold their value well. **The new shiny** is just a model-year away, and over the last two decades improvements in component weight, quality, price, and features have seen incredible increases. If you do not need (or cannot afford) to live on the bleeding edge of bike technology, the used market is the perfect place to take advantage of those that do.

In other words, you get a lot more value for your dollar on the used market. Our **KHS Tandemania** retailed for something close to $1400, yet we bought our KHS with very few miles on it for $600. Similarly, building up a new Ventana ECdM to the same spec would have been over $6,500 (plus shipping, plus tax), yet we paid $3500 for it with less than a year's ride time on it. It even came to us with brand new tires. Whether it is relatively new or well-used, maintained, and upgraded, a used tandem sale never seems to generate much more than a 50% return on the original new price.

Ebay, Craigslist, and the classified forum at MTBR.com are nationwide sales channels at your fingertips. The odds of a used tandem for sale near you are relatively low, however shipping a tandem across the country is not a huge expense and can open up your options at a more wallet-friendly price point. Now, having just finished reading about the fit-is-king mantra in **If the bike does not fit, you must acquit**, how do you make the leap to buying a used tandem that, in all likelihood, you will not be able to ride beforehand? In a word: research. In the modern day you can easily find geometry charts for the tandem in question, and if you cannot, depending on the manufacturer you can try to call them directly. Additionally, with few major tandem manufacturers, it is exceedingly likely that you can use the tandem forum on MTBR.com (or any of the handful of other mountain- or road-based tandem forums) to connect with owners of the particular bike you are looking at. You can ask them specific questions about fit, their experiences with the brand, etc.

Disadvantages to buying a used tandem includes, as mentioned above, not being able to ride it before you buy it. This is perhaps more important for a first tandem purchase, but remains an issue no matter how many tandems are in your quiver unless you are intimately familiar with the manufacturer of the bike. You also do not have a choice of components or colors – a used bike presents you with a take-it-or-leave-it decision. Buying used leaves you without warranty (see **Bigfoot down**) or the typical level of bike shop support gained when purchasing through them.

While used tandems are typically offered at a significant discount from the new price, it is not a no-brainer decision. When in doubt, post to your favorite forum and include the bike, spec, and other related information. Forum members are often willing to share their opinions on that particular bike for that particular price for your specified intended use. This can be invaluable.

Bittersweet tandem sales

As mentioned in **KHS Tandemania**, there are typically two events that spur the sale of a used tandem (however "used" it ends up being): a break-up of the tandem team or the tandem team upgrading to a new rig.

A break-up sale will typically mean that the bike is only lightly used. This is the proverbial "only driven on Sundays" condition. This is can be desirable, especially if the bike is a recent new purchase. If the break-up of the tandem team (and not of the relationship) spurred long-term storage of the tandem before its eventual sale, then a bike with few miles may still need quite a bit of reconditioning to get it into ridable shape.

Bolenas Ridge fire road, overlooking Tomales Bay in Point Reyes National Seashore. This same trail was our debut ride on our new-to-us break-up-sale ECdM back in 2008. For highlights of that trip pick up a copy of *KNOCK KNOCK! It's Carmack!* (right)

An upgrade sale, on the other hand, is an attempt to move a bike due to recent or impending purchase of a new tandem. These bikes will generally have (many) more miles on them, but also will usually have been maintained to a high standard; there is not much in the tandem world worse than being in BFE with a broken

bike, no spares on hand, with your stoker looking at you and thinking about the long hike out in clipless shoes. It is also likely that a tandem used long-term will have had a fair number of upgraded components installed over its life. These can add additional value.

The new shiny

Whether you are a long-time tandem team or are looking to buy your first tandem, there is nothing more exciting than specifying your dream tandem. We have our dream tandem in Bigfoot and bought another in Fred, yet I still drool over the shiniest of new tandem builds, with color choice being my particular fascination. While your chances of finding a road tandem at larger bike shops are not zero, even dealers for the specific manufacturer of mountain tandem you are interested in are unlikely to have one in the shop, ready to go. Tandems can be pretty expensive, with little demand to have a bike shop commit funds for a demo bike they may have a hard time selling.

What are the options? Well, it depends on the manufacturer. Take a huge, global manufacturer like Trek. While they used to make a few mid-range road tandems, currently they only offer the T900, a city/

hybrid tandem. You can pick any color as long as it is "metallic dark silver" and any frame size as long as it is "18.5," which does not translate directly to any particular measurement on the geometry chart Trek supplies (though it should be seat tube length). For Trek, one size fits all.

At the other end of the options spectrum is a company like Ventana. Ventana pride themselves on being a small, independent bike manufacturer, and take particular pride with their tandem lineup. While small and independent, they offer more than 50 different tandem frames (four tire sizes, all but the fat-tandem size available in eight standard geometries and with or without S&S couplers) as standard.

If you want custom geometry, they will accommodate for an up-charge (an additional fee). Standard color selection? 17! Want a specific powder coat color? For an up-charge they will buy in the specific powder and coat your frame. When we talked with Ventana about our S&S ECdM, we were directed to a powder coat supplier's website to choose our color from hundreds of offerings.

Road tandem manufacturers like Co-Motion and Calfee will, again, boggle your mind with the options available.

Most other manufacturers are going to be somewhere between Trek's single offering and the unlimited combinations Ventana ultimately offers.

Then there is the burgeoning adventure tandem arena. Also known as gravel grinders, these are basically road frames modified to take wider tires, racks, and lights (see **Tour de gravel**). Co-Motion is the heavy-hitter in this category with their Java and Mocha lines. As with Ventana, Co-Motion can do custom geometry and custom features. Need a longer stoker compartment and cable-tie braze-ons to run full brake- and shifter-cable housing? No problem.

Where do you start to narrow down manufacturers? The easy way is to decide on the type of tandem you and your partner are interested in (see **Tandemachina**). Most teams will not ride exclusively on either dirt or road, but each type of tandem is somewhat-to-fairly adaptable to different terrain. We have ridden Bigfoot on the road and short rides I preferred it to our Burley. We had ridden the Burley off-road and, while I did not prefer it on dirt in the slightest, it had always sprouted thoughts of a road tandem with bigger tires. I took the Burley to the limit with 35mm cyclocross tires, but the Co-Motion with 700x54mm tires opened up a new level of comfort on the road and sprouted new rides and new experiences on existing rides.

For whatever type of tandem you decide on, there will be specific manufacturers to look at and choose between. Your choice may be influenced by a bike shop having a particular tandem on the floor to demo (see **If the bike does not fit, you must acquit**), and this is no small issue if you have never ridden tandem before. While we bought our Burley from a local dealer, we ordered the Ventana and Co-Motion directly from the manufacturers as there were no dealers within hours of us.

When the subject of new tandems comes up, there is invariably some cringing at the prices some of these bikes achieve. Years down the road (or trail), the initial cost will pale against the return on investment gained by getting out and riding, truly, with your partner.

Order up

How does one go about ordering a custom tandem? For us, it mostly involved calling up the manufacturer directly. As tandeming is a niche itself, the companies that make custom tandems are not the big conglomerates owned by Gigante MegaCorp. Quite often, in our experience, ordering a custom tandem brings you in direct contact with the owner.

For Ventana that was the case, as mentioned in **Ventana El Conquistador de Montañas**. While our S&S frame was custom, the geometry was one of the standard sizes, matching the geometry of our original Ventana. As such, the conversation was more straight-forward, consisting mainly of the color choice and discussions of the steel material choice (see **New Bigfoot rising**).

Co-Motion has a sales side of the house, however any custom tandem order puts you in contact with the president, who is also the chief designer. My stoker had a few phone conversations with him during the drawings of our frame, and actually had to convince him that what we really wanted was the extended stoker cockpit we had originally asked for. His impression was that my stoker is taller than the average tandem stoker,

but part of the Co-Motion process is entering each of our dimensional information into their fit sheet, which, theoretically, they take into consideration during an assessment of frame options.

We thought that hurdle was cleared, and signed off on a frame drawing showing an extended stoker cockpit - the maximum that would still fit into the S&S cases. Then the hard part arrived, or so we thought: the wait. We placed our order at the end of January and did not see our new bike arrive until early May - and this was Co-Motion's slow season.

You can imagine our disappointment when my stoker looked at her new, limo-length stoker cockpit and went straight to the measuring tape. She came up with a measurement of ~28.5" which, if you have been reading through this book front-to-back, you know to be the measurement of the standard Co-Motion Java frame. Indeed, through some fluke at Co-Motion, they ended up building and shipping us a standard Java. Oops.

This was not discovered until after business hours on Friday, so I composed a long e-mail documenting not only the dimensional issues but also some cable management concerns I had (placement of cable stops, certain routing and rubbing issues) and sent it off. We did not get an immediate call Monday morning from Co-Motion; instead my stoker made a few calls to finally contact the sales staff.

They were apologetic about the sizing mistake, but not terribly concerned about my issues with their cable management. However, as compensation for having to send the tandem back, Co-Motion did accommodate my desired corrections to their cable routings. We just wanted the tandem we ordered, and wanted that tandem to live for many years without unnecessary wear points.

The second bike we received five weeks later showed 30.5" between crank centers and marked improvements in cable management. Upon a quick measurement of the largest frame section, followed by bike disassembly to verify, I could not help but notice that this frame section did not have a hope of fitting into the S&S case. This was problematic on a number of levels.

Further discussion with Co-Motion indicated Frame #2 was not built to the design plan and not caught by QC following fabrication. After more discussion, it was agreed that Frame #3 would be built for us, again at no (additional) charge.

You have a lot more room to customize a bike you order from Ventana, Co-Motion, Calfee, or other custom bike manufacturer. You will, however, have to pay closer attention when ordering custom to verify the result meets your expectations.

Wide load

Once you and your partner have a tandem to ride, how do you get it to the start of the trailhead, bike path, or road loop? All manner of vehicle has been used to transport tandems (including a motorcycle!), but the two obvious choices are by car or by pickup truck.

If by car, the most common way to transport a tandem is by using an external bike rack (think Thule or Yakima) on the roof. Availability of tandem-specific bike rails (required as tandems are feet longer than a single bike) varies with the year and the brand, but the most popular is the "pivot" style tandem rail. In this style you would remove the front wheel, lift the fork up to the rail, and secure it in a bike clamp. Then you lift the rear and pivot it onto the rear portion of the rail.

Tandem-specific bike rails, however, are not available to fit all cars. Smaller cars with shorter roofs will not be able to support a tandem's length. In those cases, you may be able to fit the bike inside the car, but there will be disassembly required, up to removing both wheels and handlebars, before it will fit inside cars or small SUVs.

For those with larger SUVs, using a suitable hitch rack will allow you to carry a tandem on the back of your vehicle. One suggestion here would be to strap the front wheel sideways so it cannot swing out while you drive.

We transport tandems by pickup truck. My stoker brought a Toyota Tacoma into our marriage, and it is a near-perfect tandem transportation device. For shorter trips, or trips in which the tandem is the only thing in the bed, I drop the tailgate, lay the bike down on its side, and strap it in. For longer trips I made two different racks that fit in the bed and secure one or two tandems upright, after removing the front wheels.

Road and mountain tandems shown secured to a custom rack.

Since we mostly ride off-road and have trails available to us a quarter-mile from our door, nine times out of ten we simply ride from our doorstep.

Coupling couplers

In **New Bigfoot rising** I talked about a coupled tandem. How would that change your transportation options? As discussed, it would allow you to break down your long bike into two airline-approved suitcases. This makes for much easier packaging into an SUV or, possibly, crammed into the backseat of a mid-size car.

Key to this is the "airline-approved suitcases" bit. With these, and your bike packed just so, you can travel the world with your bike. The cases are within the dimensional limits for airline checked baggage without incurring oversize fees, and when packed with a tandem fall within the standard weight restrictions as well.

It takes a bit of creative packing to get a full-suspension mountain tandem into two cases, but it can be done. If you are traveling via airline, I recommend using cable ties (aka zip ties) to connect the contents of each case to itself. TSA is going to be interested in your cases and

when (not if) they open them, you want the contents to remain as you packed it during their inspection.

During one of your packing attempts, take pictures and make notes. Each of our cases contains a list of what parts go in each case and a set of padding specific for those pieces is stored within.

Half a bike in one case...

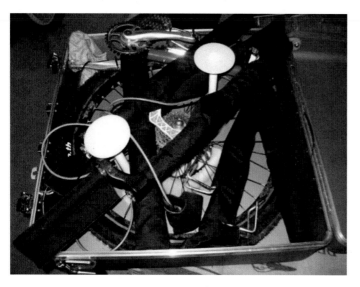

Half a bike in the other case...

The main issue with transporting your tandem in pieces is that you will need a place and tools to reassemble the bike at your destination. This is rarely convenient and, in some cases, may prove to be a bigger hassle than its ultimate worth. My wife and I have dreamed up two train-based vacations that were not taken because the logistics did not pan out. AMTRAK requires tandems to be boxed, so while the Southwest Chief stops in the mountain biking Mecca of Winter Park, Colorado,

arriving with a bike in pieces has put a damper on those plans.

Our schedules finally allowed us to attend an AORTA event (see **Mark Twain National Forest**) and the couplers on Bigfoot allowed us to bring our bike across the country to the event.

Upon reassembly, the only travel/TSA-related issue was a pinched shifter cable. I was able to tune around it during our AORTA adventure, but I carry a spare just in case. Upon our return home I discovered a bent brake rotor*, which was able to be trued. Hey, there is a first time for everything. For what is involved, I consider that a pretty good outcome.

While we had an entire deck to reassemble Bigfoot, it was still a challenge.

*If you are reading this book in preparation for ordering the tandem of your dreams, and your dreams include traveling (and, hence, couplers), I would strongly suggest looking at wheels with the Shimano Centerlock hubs/brake rotors. This would enable a much easier removal of the rotors during transportation in the cases, and eliminating one more potential issue at your destination.

Turning it up to 11

Once you and your partner spend some time in the saddles, you will get over the initial troubles and tribulations of riding tandem. Your roles will be understood by both the captain and the stoker. Your expectations of each member of the team are known and, in the main, fulfilled. Early communication issues will be sorted and new words created to solve problems as you ride in the years ahead.

That level of comfort and confidence on the bike just means that you are ready to take your riding to the next level. Now, if that sounds like a bunch of promotional-speaker malarkey, it is, but there is also a wide world of terrain (both paved and dirt) waiting beyond the comfort of the protected bike path or flat, wide fireroad. Since biking is freedom, do not be constrained by what you know. If you did that, you would never have gotten on a tandem in the first place.

Tandem SMASH!

After a few weeks of riding tandem, you will have realized one of the bigger limitations of your new bike, whether you decided on a road tandem or went with a mountain tandem: riding over anything but smooth pavement is a controlled crash. Given the physics of a tandem's long wheelbase and heavy weights at each end, it should not be too surprising that popping the front wheel up and over an obstacle is not going to happen.

On the road you can accommodate for this by never getting into a situation where you need to lift the front wheel. This means the captain needs to avoid road debris and the larger potholes. But this also means that at times you will have to stop and dismount to clear an obstacle such as a gated entry into a park or a curb in front of a store or restaurant.

Off the road, the obstacle issues are part of the fun, but no less impossible to wheelie over. The benefit most mountain tandems have over their road brethren is that you can "pump" the suspension fork to help clear short, blunt obstacles. The pump technique involves approaching the obstacle (say a street curb or low wooden barrier at the trailhead), bouncing your body to compress the fork, then having the fork rebound just as the front tire hits the obstacle. This action gets the front of the tandem slightly higher and slightly lighter than it would normally be, and also allows absorption of the hit by the entire travel of your fork (instead of the travel left over after sag). Granted, it is not much, but combined with the typical mountain tandem front tire, it is a world of difference compared to trying to clearing a curb on a road tandem.

If you come up to an obstacle that is much taller than a street curb, however, the pump trick does not help enough, and you have to be riding all the faster in order to maintain momentum to get up and over. These higher-speed impacts are something I avoid for my sake, the sake of my stoker, and for the sake of our bike. Plowing into a blunt object at high(er) speed is just a recipe to break parts, and hopefully none of those are body parts. Obstacles like rocky step-ups that you know you can clean on your single bike may be otherwise impossible if you cannot get your body weight over the rear wheel and lots of air under the front wheel. That does not happen on a tandem under anything considered "controlled" circumstances.

Stand and deliver

Standing on a tandem is no problem. Call out "coast," wait for your partner to respond, then stand up out of the saddle and sigh with relief. If you wanted to pedal out of the saddle, however, that is another thing entirely. My wife and I practiced pedaling out of the saddle a year or so after we bought the Burley. When planned for, it was mildly successful. We were able to pedal up a steep hill in a gear one or two higher than if we were seated.

That success paled in comparison to how we would have climbed that same hill on single bikes. On a tandem, as always, you need to compromise your riding styles towards an average, and this includes how much you swing the bike back and forth when climbing out of the saddle. I approach this fairly aggressively, having grown up on BMX bikes where pumping the bars as you accelerate is part of the technique. My stoker grew up on road bikes and very rarely stood up to pedal, and when she did she kept her bar movements to a minimum. I found it very cramped and unnatural to stand and pedal while trying to keep bar movements to a minimum. Combine that with the slightly flexy nature of the Burley and it affected my power output and my desire to stand and pedal at all.

On a mountain tandem, you can stand and pedal in similar conditions – uphill over non-technical terrain. I have seen it on YouTube and when done properly it looks like ballet. Typical mountain tandem gearing eliminates any need to stand and pedal on flats or downhills; we can top out our gearing on flat dirt terrain. During the times we need the power of pedaling out of the saddle we are typically in steep, loose, technical conditions. Trying to clear this sort of trail with peaky "power" pedaling would cause a lack of traction at the back (stoker's weight is off the seat) right as another power pulse hit as the pedals go over again.

With practice, pedaling out of the saddle on a tandem will feel as natural as doing the same on a single bike. In reality, especially as half our team was not much of a stand-and-pedal kind of rider, we have not tried it in 10 years.

Traffic cop

Your stoker has a lot of freedom to look around while riding. Since your stoker cannot look ahead, looking around is all that is left! As a team you can use your stoker's freedom to your benefit in situations where there is road traffic, such as on a road ride or while riding to the trailhead. Being able to turn around fully and spend seconds examining traffic conditions is a huge safety improvement over the milliseconds we would allow ourselves to take eyes off the road on single bikes.

Additionally, you will find that traffic is much more accommodating of cyclists on a tandem than you might be used to as single riders. In the last half-dozen years we have shifted most of our riding to the dirt, but this can still involve a couple miles of road riding to the trailhead depending on our start point. Having a car let you make a left, being able to keep eyes on them the entire time, and then giving them a full wave afterwards is a role only a tandem stoker has the time or ability to fulfill. Long live the tandem stoker!

While the captain can continue to pay attention to road or trail conditions and keep the **Rubber-side down**, the stoker can acknowledge passing cyclists, say "hi" to hikers or pedestrians, and generally be public relations for you.

You turn me right 'round baby

The most common statement we hear on the trail is some version of "She's not pedaling!" The most common question is some version of "You don't take that thing on singletrack, do you?" Of course we do! Singletrack is the best. "Well, what about switchbacks?!" Switchbacks are not the barrier that most people think.

In my experience, there is nothing I can do, ride, or clean on a single bike that I cannot do while captaining a tandem. This excepts wheelies and bunnyhops but includes switchbacks. Now, maybe this means I am sort of rubbish on a single bike, but teams ride mountain tandems all over the world in all conditions and terrains. When we answer that we ride all the trails in **Point Mugu State Park**, which include a few with dozens of switchbacks among them, they look shocked.

Now, we do not clean every switchback every time. Trail conditions change over time and our local trails get "maintained" somewhat often by the local trail advocacy crew. A switchback that was cleanable one week might need a dab next month or a dismount

the month after. In the end, the only way to clean a switchback is to try.

Obviously there is technique to cleaning a switchback. This is compounded by the fact that everyone is different. Switchbacks constructed these days are smoother, have better transitions, and generally describe a wider arc. If you have a trail system with modern multi-use trails, switchbacks found there would be perfect to practice on.

After you discuss your version of the verbal code "switch," approach the switchback in an appropriate gear for the gradient and stay wide. Visually check the switchback, looking for rocks or ruts that would knock you off your desired line or cause you to lose traction. The ideal turn will run the front wheel wide of the apex while keeping the rear wheel on the solid trailbed of the switchback.

There are generally two things that stop a tandem negotiating a cleanable switchback. The first is inappropriate speed, and this can be either too fast **or** too slow. Switchbacks need controlled momentum to clean as you are usually fighting the tight turn, a

As you approach the switchback, call out "switch" for your stoker, assess the corner, and steer the widest arc possible.

The inside of a switchback will often be a low spot, so loose dirt and rocks collect here, making it very loose. You want to keep the rear tire out of loose portions of the switchback if possible.

Continue to sight your line through the switchback, as often you will not be able to see through the entire corner before you are in the middle of it. Keep your front tire as wide as possible and start thinking about powering out of the turn.

Once you can see the trail straighten ahead and you know your steering has been sharp enough to make the switchback, call out "go" to signal to your stoker to resume normal power!

gradient change, and a loose surface all in the same corner. Conversely, if the stoker is putting down too much power, the tandem will push straight through the back of the corner and no amount of steering will fix the problem.

The second barrier to cleaning a switchback is a lack of traction. Switchbacks see their fair share of erosion by water and by skidding mountain bikers, so traction is always a problem. Spinning the rear tire here will mean a dab.

Once we get through most of the switchback I will tell my stoker "go." This point in the switchback is usually where I have run the front tire wide and it is trying to climb the side of the trail. The additional power from my stoker helps keep our momentum to finish the switchback on two wheels. Occasionally the turn is precarious enough that I do not have the time to call out "go." I just start pedaling like mad to keep it going. Your stoker will need to be prepared for this, which should be part of the agreed definition of "switch."

Switchbacks require practice. They are not an impossible obstacle, no matter what every single-bike rider assumes.

Two-way street

Often singletrack is tight with poor sight lines. That is part of what we love about it. However, when you encounter a rider or riders coming the opposite way and you meet them head-on, they only see you. They do not see your stoker. What is more, they do not expect your stoker. The oncoming riders see a mountain bike and automatically assume it is a single bike. So if they "go high" to pass you at speed, they may plan to get back on the trailbed where your stoker is.

This has rarely been an issue as most riders will yield if you are riding uphill. When it has been an issue it has been a higher-speed affair that could have consequences for your stoker. If you encounter a rider coming at you from the opposite direction and he (sorry, but it has always been a "he") is not showing signs of slowing or signs that he sees you are a team of two, duck or move to the side to show off your stoker. Even if this does not slow him down, he is at least aware of your long bike. Sometimes it is the best you can hope for.

Up, up, and away

It was nine years into our mountain tandem adventures before we caught actual air on a ride. We rode Whoops trail in Bend but only ever got one wheel or the other off the ground at any one time. Tandems are too long, with too much weight aboard, to catch air where a single bike would catch air. If you are at the point in your riding where you are contemplating air, think about the style of jump **and** the speed necessary to get both tires off the ground at the same time. I tried for air when I thought it was safe, but even safe kickers were too abrupt to get air under both tires.

What it took was speed and a gentle yump. Not a jump, but a fairly large grade reversal built by California State Parks across the width of a fireroad. We had come down the fireroad plenty of times before, but what usually was just an exciting bump for my stoker turned into actual air. It was the gentlest of motions, but the brief feeling of weightlessness was pure amazing. The landing was equally plush thanks to the suspension. With the trail ahead clear I turned quickly to my stoker and grinned, she giggled in reply.

Rubber-side up

We have ridden thousands of miles on our tandems. We have crashed. While my stoker trusts me to keep the **Rubber-side down**, there is no guarantee. None of our falls were the result of me riding dangerously. None of these crashes caused injury, and only one resulted in mechanical issues. The lack of injury does not really make up for the fact that I had just dropped my stoker on the ground. It is not that much better from my stoker's point of view, as she has to watch me go down.

Our only road fall of note was so many years ago, at such low speed, of such suddenness, and of such little consequence that the details have been lost to time. It was early in our road-tandeming days, and involved crossing an intersection from a stop sign then making an immediate left turn. I must not have got the pedals correctly oriented for the turn and probably struck one or both inside pedals on the road (see **Ten-four good buddy/Pedal up**). This knocked the bike off the line I had chosen and sent me straight towards the curb. One ham-fisted brake grab combined with not getting my foot down in time led us to the ground. No harm, we just picked ourselves up, dusted off, and got back on.

Off-road falls have been more numerous, but at this point so have off-road miles ridden. I can readily recount four falls of note. The first occurred on a turn in the trail, but to this day I do not know the actual cause. I assume I steered into a very loose patch of dirt and the front wheel washed out. One second I was riding along and making the turn for the corner at fairly normal speed, the next second I was helping my stoker up off the ground. The motion of the handlebars during the washout bashed the rear shifter into the ground, breaking its case. We got off the mountain with some captain's trail rash and a dangling shifter, but otherwise no worse for wear. Tough to learn a lesson from a fall that happened before I could react, though.

The last indignity occurred after some trail maintenance by our local trail advocacy crew. While I am a fan of trail maintenance and have helped build local trails, the fairly regular actions of this local crew amount to trail vandalism as much as anything approaching maintenance. The trail in question entered a series of S curves, with the one turn in particular featuring a two-foot-high berm. The trail crew had come in and knocked down the taller foot off the berm and left the resulting loose dirt scattered over the trailbed. They love doing that. The trouble was, while they had knocked down the top half of the berm they left the hard lip of the remaining berm covered in loose dirt. Along comes Team Bigfoot and the front tire plowed through the loose top, hit the hard lip of the lower part of the berm, and kept going straight. We as riders were already into our lean around the S turn as normal. We went down into a creek bed below. Again, no real harm, but the trailwork was most foul.

Take the trail conditions under any section of loose fill with a grain of salt. And if you do drop your stoker on the ground, gentlemen, resist the natural urge to make sure the bike is okay – check on your stoker first!

Parts is parts

Tandems are harder on parts than single road or mountain bikes. You have double the power being put through the same drivetrain and double the weight on the wheels. I also, easily, make double the shifts during a ride compared to riding my single bike. This is just a factor of trying to keep two people happy with the gear selection, an unenviable task that gives the shifters and derailleurs a workout.

All of which is to say that low-quality components are unlikely to last long enough for the financial savings to be realized. If you are buying a used tandem, or a new tandem off the bike shop floor, look for bikes with at least mid-level components all around. If buying new, do not skimp here only to realize a part failure 10 miles from home.

Easy is the road

While the above is absolutely as true for road tandems as for mountain tandems, our road tandem experience has either been very lucky or it has just made the case for quality components from the beginning. Our

Burley Duet featured the original Shimano 105 brifters, cranks, and front derailleur, Shimano hubs, and Shimano XT cassette and rear derailleur (for the 11-34T gearing out back) for the vast majority of its life. We finally wore out the right shift lever after 13 years of riding.

For heavier teams, look to gravel-grinder equipment (tires, wheels, forks, oh my) if you are encountering durability issues. Given our issues on trail, I would have expected the Burley's rear hub to have imploded long before we sold the bike on, yet it was working as fine as ever. Since we never climb 15% gradients in granny gear, the road hub never sees the kind of torque we are capable of putting down.

What a drag

Most newer tandems are moving to disc brakes, which eliminates the heat-induced failures possible with rim brakes. For those tandems still fitted with rim brakes, examine the rear hub to see if the non-drive side is threaded. If so, you can add an Arai drag brake.

The Arai drag brake, as fitted to our **Burley Duet**.

The bar-end shifter to actuate the drag brake.

The original Arai is no longer in production, but there has been a re-creation made available in addition to the various eBay offerings of used or NOS drag brakes. Drag brake use is a fraction of ride time, so even used parts will likely have many road miles left.

To complete the drag brake installation, you will need to add a way to engage the brake when desired. Since the Burley came with brifters, I added an Ultegra bar-end shifter set for index shifting.

This allows me to reach down, set the appropriate amount of drag, and get both hands back on the bars. When installing a drag brake, remember to pack the tools necessary to remove the cable from the brake and the brake arm from the frame. You will not be able to remove the rear wheel with these things still attached.

Steep is the mountain

Durability issues really reign their ugly heads when riding steep trails off road. Our own parts failures have only involved snapping chains and imploding rear hubs, but other teams have folded cassette cogs and timing rings among other failures. Similar to the advice given in **Easy is the road**, mountain tandem teams can raid the downhill (DH) parts bins for wheels, tires, forks, etc.

Boom goes the hub

Chain failure can be fixed in five minutes with a chain tool and a SRAM Powerlink (you are packing spares, right?), but hub issues can really ruin your ride. Ask me how I know! Of the three in-ride hub failures, my favorite story has us climbing Guadalasco trail in **Point Mugu State Park**. This is twisty singletrack with a couple of g-out creek crossings, eight or nine tight switchback turns, and almost 1,000 feet of elevation gain over four miles. There's lots of up here. One particular steep section had us powering up like mad, only to hear an ominous grunch. Pedaling still worked, so we continued to the top of the rise, then came to an inelegant stop due to not being able to freewheel.

A quick diagnosis strongly suggested our full-suspension mountain tandem had become a fixie. We could change gears and pedal forward, we could pedal backward (that would be a trick), but we could not freewheel. So we could not coast and we could not back pedal to set up for an obstacle. On tight, twisty singletrack eight miles in the boonies.

Thinking it was probably better to start heading home, we turned the tandem around and started riding back while we still could. The hub was completely silent at this point, but pedaling did produce forward motion. With a fixie, however, riding downhill was a trick to keep up with the speed. I grabbed a lot of brake while descending and had to pay all the more attention to the trail ahead so I could get in the right gear and have the pedals in the right spots to tackle obstacles. The g-out creek crossings were also interesting since there was no coasting full-speed into the g-out already in the right gear to climb out of it – we had to be in granny gear heading in, pedaling (slowly) the entire time.

It was an interesting ride for my stoker and I. Without being able to coast or freewheel, we stopped a couple times just to stretch out. The entire ride back we were plotting how to upgrade our wheels, for this was the third rear hub implosion in 18 months. We were able to ride out after two of them, but a third left us a 10-mile walk home after we split apart the hub shell. While the hub brand had stood up to a lot of other tandem teams, this was little comfort for us. $700 was exchanged for a new pair of hoops laced with Chris King hubs, and years and tons of miles later we have never had a further issue.

Component musings

While you can bolt any component on to your tandem, some (particularly forks) may be tandem-rated by the manufacturer. Which means that some will not be tandem-rated. What does this really mean? Tandem-rated components are those for which the manufacturer will cover warranty issues when used on a tandem. Fox infamously refuses to rate any of their forks for tandem use, so dealers and distributors cannot equip tandems with Fox forks. Now, individual teams can (and have) elect to buy and install a Fox fork onto their tandem, but warranty issues quickly become opaque without lying about the original application.

Tandem-rating does not really extend into most parts of a tandem (bars, seats, shifters, cranks), but even the legendary Chris King hubs have a tandem-rated option (steel driveshell being the main difference). Experience from the tandem population at large can help steer you to suitable parts beyond what the manufacturer says, but keep in mind those manufacturers have reasons why they are not rating their parts for tandem use.

Maintenance schedule

My mountain tandem maintenance schedule baffles most of my single-bike friends. I replace drive chains every six months during which we are lucky to put 1,000 miles on the bike. I completely service the Chris King rear hub every year, and I even bought the service tool to do so. Chainrings and cassettes get replaced approximately every 18 months. Conversely, I go six to seven years between chains on my single bike.

My road tandem experience is much more basic, and matches closer to single road bike norms. Road bikes are not generally subject to the same dirt and grit environments, so drivetrain components last longer. Road bikes are ridden on flatter, or at least more rolling terrain, than the steep ups and downs on a backcountry trail in SoCal, so chains last longer as well.

Initially I had to have a bike shop do all this work as I thought getting a rear derailleur to shift correctly was a black art. But taking a tandem to the bike shop is not quite as simple as it is with a single bike. And, strangely, I found that most bike shops could not do quality wrenching on a tandem. Tandems are not really different front single bikes where it counts (drivetrain tuning), but picking up the bike only to have to take it back for rework started to get my goat.

Combine that frustration with the turn-around time if we broke something and it added up to significant time off the bike. I eventually bought some bike tools and stocked all the wear parts, then started honing my innate mechanical skill to the art of bicycle maintenance. This has the added benefit of making me somewhat more useful when something breaks or needs adjustment on the trail.

Split ends

One tip I will share for both road and mountain tandems is to buy and install a pair of cable splitters into the shifter cables. Likely you do not have an S&S-coupled tandem, so why do you need cable splitters? Installing cable splitters allows you to use standard single bike-length shifter cables. Without cable splitters you need to find a bike shop with tandem-length cables. Standard-length shifter cables are available everywhere all the time, and you can buy one length for your tandems and single bikes.

Mountain tandems park any damn where. (right)

On a day-long ride through upper Bend, Oregon, west of Phil's Trail System, we had lunch at a ski hut in the Dechutes National Forest. (following page, left)

At the top of Whoops trail in Phil's Trail System, Bend, Oregon. (following page, right)

NO

PARKING

Ticket to ride

With a tandem and a willing partner, where can you take your new bike to have a great time on two wheels? If you live in California, or want to visit California, I have some great spots on road and off, and many locations have both so you can double your fun doubling your fun. These are all places we can vouch for as great tandem riding, beginning on the road.

17 Mile Drive (road)

17 Mile Drive is a gated community that lies between Pacific Grove and Carmel along the coast of Central California. It encompasses multi-million dollar mansions, Pebble Beach, and the 1%, alongside some of the most beautiful coastal scenery in the world. Your stoker will be agog at things to see and people to watch.

> 17 Mile Drive, at one of the many scenic turnouts. The scenery must be seen to be believed; quintessential Central Coast. (left)

We prefer to stay in Pacific Grove when visiting the Monterey Bay area. If you have read *KNOCK KNOCK!* *It's Carmack!*, then you know our current favorite B&B is the Old St. Angela Inn in Pacific Grove. The B&B is situated one block inland from the Monterey Bay Coastal Trail (MBCT), a paved and separated 10-mile bike path connecting Pacific Grove to Marina, CA. If you turn left at the Pacific Grove terminus of the MBCT and ride on Ocean View Blvd. around the north tip of Pacific Grove, you may think you are already on 17 Mile Drive given the views, mansions, and golf courses.

17 Mile Drive itself begins at the Pacific Grove Gate at the intersection of 17 Mile Drive and Sunset Drive. While people in cars are stuck paying the $10 to get in, bicycles have their own free pass through the gated entry.

17 Mile Drive is very beautiful to look at, but 99.9% of drivers will also be looking, so it can be a bit nerve-wracking to ride along the partial-to-zero shoulder amongst the traffic. Should you venture onto 17 Mile Drive during one of the busier days (weekends, or any day during summer), our suggestion would be to ride it opposite of the majority of traffic. 17 Mile Drive has five gates, but from the Pacific Grove Gate most people will follow signs pointing to a right-hand turn

for 17 Mile Drive. If, instead, you go straight at that intersection and head for Sloat Road to Lopez Road, you will be making a loop on 17 Mile Drive that is the opposite of most everyone else. 17 Mile Drive loop has a line painted onto the roadway, making it impossible to get lost.

Lopez Road leads to a nice, quiet ride through the forest, with most of the scenery hidden away. You will eventually end up on Sunridge Road as it approaches Highway 68 at another 17 Mile Drive gate. Turn right to stay on 17 Mile Drive before exiting the gate and continue south towards Carmel. At Carmel Way you can turn off into the city of Carmel for food, drink, and people watching, or continue on 17 Mile Drive as it turns back north. Making a left onto Cypress Drive will be your clue that the scenery is about to get real. The following miles will be full of cliffsides, shoreline, lone cypress trees, and large skin bags of snorting mammals…and then there are the sea lions!

Eventually you will retrace your steps to the Pacific Grove Gate. Continue back to Pacific Grove and a well-earned ice cream cone at the Ice Cream Shoppe!

Fort Ord National Monument (mountain)

You could ride 17 Mile Drive on a mountain tandem, but you could not ride at Ford Ord on a road tandem. Fort Ord National Monument is a mostly-retired US Army base and home to the annual Sea Otter Classic mountain bike event. Approximately half of the original base is still restricted due to ongoing munitions cleanup, however the other half of the base is overseen by the Bureau of Land Management, and mountain bikes are welcome.

In looking at the free, detailed trail map, the ridable portion of Fort Ord can be divided into "north" and "south" sections. The south section is where most of the cross-country races are held during Sea Otter, and these trails are mainly fire roads, with some sections of singletrack in between. The scenery and riding is very Southern California, and while we have ridden there, we do not prefer it over many trail systems in SoCal.

What we do prefer, mightily, is the north section of Fort Ord. Though smaller in size, this area is nearly all singletrack of the tight and fun variety. Many of the trails are relatively short, but at the conclusion of one trail you are almost always at a junction where three or four other trails begin. This can lead to a wonderfully improvisational ride where you start on one trail and then keep taking a right, then a left and each trail junction. With a map, it is impossible to get lost, and you can never get very far from the core concentration of trails. If you ever read the juvenile (sorry, "young adult") Choose Your Own Adventure books, Fort Ord North is just like that.

Whatever combination of trails you ride (by happenstance, or otherwise), ensure you hit trails 61 and 62. Repeatedly. We generally aim in the direction of 61/62 and once there we session those two trails multiple times. They never get old. 61/62 are tight, twisty singletrack that perfectly accommodate the length of a well-ridden tandem. The trails are smooth and free of sand (something to watch for in parts of Fort Ord North), and most days the number of other mountain bikers you will pass can be counted by your stoker on one hand.

Point Reyes Lighthouse (road)

Readers of *KNOCK KNOCK! It's Carmack!* know we love Olema, CA and Point Reyes National Seashore. A great weekday road ride from Olema or Point Reyes Station is to take Sir Frances Drake Blvd. north along the west side of Tomales Bay, on an out-and-back loop to Point Reyes Lighthouse. From Olema it is a little over 40 miles round-trip, with the promise of stopping at Bovine Bakery, Cowgirl Creamery, or the Pine Cone Diner.

Sir Frances Drake Blvd. is a narrow two-lane that is the only way to Point Reyes Lighthouse. The lighthouse is closed from December through March every year, so check hours before visiting. Due to the narrow nature of the roadway, we suggest riding out on a weekday. We have done it on weekends without issue and the road conditions are perfectly manageable. As noted in 17 Mile Drive, we are somewhat traffic adverse when said traffic is comprised of touristy looky-loo's.

The route is simple so the description is short, but this is no reflection on the incredible scenery in store. Time it right and there will be ample whale watching to be done from the lighthouse as well. Pack a lunch!

Irvine Regional Park (mountain)

Irvine Regional Park (IRP), tucked in suburban Orange County, California, seems like another world once you are out of the IRP parking lot and headed north on Roadrunner Loop Trail. You leave the housing sprawl behind, though its remnants remain on far-flung ridges. As captain, you will not have time to notice. Find your way to Chute Trail, the trail hinted at in **You turn me right 'round baby** as the perfect place to come to master switchbacks.

IRP trails are built following the modern playbook for trail construction. They are smooth, well maintained, and the switchbacks are wide enough (just) for tandems to clean them with just a little practice and experience. If possible, follow a local tandem team around and pick up tricks and tips. We were invited to IRP to ride with Team Zibell, and following their lead led me to take the switchbacks wide, including running the front wheel wide at the end. This was key for IRP's switchbacks.

IRP gets hot in summer and there is no shade, so carry sufficient water before setting off. A hot ride at IRP led me to upgrade my CamelBak to a bigger bladder, and that was complimenting the water bottles we also carried. Just a testament to how many miles we spun around IRP having a blast on their challenging terrain.

Ventura River Trail (road)

Ventura River Trail is a segregated bike path leaving the coast city of Ventura, CA, and heading north towards the granola haven of Ojai, CA. Between the two cities is approximately 20 miles of easy, protected bike path, perfect for the beginning or traffic-adverse tandem teams.

VRT actually begins at the corner of Rex and Dubbers Streets, just off West Main Street. You can add the Ventura Promenade to this out-and-back by starting your ride in the Pierpont community surrounding Pierpont Blvd. and Seaward Ave. We lived nearby when we bought our **Burley Duet**, and VRT was the perfect out-and-back loop to ride while learning how to be a tandem team.

The first section from the beach to Foster Park is flat; between Foster Park and Libby Park in Ojai the trail climbs 1000 feet or so. Foster Park is a great pit stop for bathroom and rest. The gradient is never excessive as the trail gains elevation over 15 miles, but the return trip back to the beach is quite a bit faster than the uphill run into Ojai.

Our usual destination is Libby Park in Ojai, a central community park just across the street from shopping and surrounded by restaurants. We typically brown bag it, but Libby Park offers benches, shade, and grass for your dining pleasure. We have even been known to find some shaded grass and take a quick nap.

As mentioned in Burley Duet, VRT suffers slightly from pavement wear and tear, mainly from tree roots. There are a couple sections that are particularly bumpy on a road tandem as a result, so make sure your stoker's seat post is better than basic and keep both hands on the handlebars up front. Not all of the bumps are easy to see when doing 25 mph+. Aside from weekend mornings, traffic on VRT is very light, with few walkers or other cyclists, and the trail is well-sighted, so typical road riding speeds are easy to attain and maintain.

Point Mugu State Park (mountain)

Point Mugu State Park is better known as Sycamore Canyon and is located in the western Santa Monica Mountains National Recreation Area in Southern California. The "Sycamore Canyon" shorthand is due to the many sycamore trees in the canyon and because the main canyon road through the park is known as Sycamore Canyon Fireroad (see also **Newbury Park Surf Loop**). Spreading over eight miles between Newbury Park on the north end and the Pacific Ocean on the south end, the bike-legal trails also spread westward a few miles, resulting in a large and variable mountain bike playfield.

There are flat fireroads, steep and short fireroads, long fireroads with 1100 feet of elevation gain over 3.5 miles (or 1100 feet of descent, depending on which way you ride it), and tighter, flowy fireroads that descend a few hundred feet over a few miles. At the end of the day, however, the fireroads, no matter how flowy, just lead you to the sweet Point Mugu singletrack.

There's the Sin Nombre/Big Sycamore/Two Foxes trifecta, a more-or-less flatter set of singletrack that runs parallel to Sycamore Canyon Fireroad. There's Guadalasco, four miles of twisting singletrack climbing 1000 feet and featuring nine switchbacks to practice on. As of this writing (2018) the switchbacks are in decent shape and cleanable by teams familiar with the techniques mentioned in **You turn me right 'round baby**, or teams familiar with the trail itself. There is also Wood Canyon Vista (also known as Backbone), a shorter climb (two miles, 740 feet of gain) to the same ridgeline as Guadalasco. Backbone has only one sharp switchback that varies due to surface prep – sometimes we can clean it, other times we cannot.

We live a quarter-mile away from a trail that will deliver us into a National Park Service-managed open space (Rancho Sierra Vista) that delivers us into Point Mugu State Park. With that route we can ride from our house to the trailhead and then spend the next 11 miles riding off-road all the way to the Pacific Ocean. We have to cross one narrow two-lane backroad, but that is a small price to pay.

On a Mountain Bike Unit volunteer trail patrol at the north end of Point Mugu State Park with Mt. Boney peak rising behind us. (right) Photo credit: Buz Fulton.

With trails to match your skill level and to keep you honest, coupled with the experience of riding to the beach, Point Mugu State Park offers a lot as a weekend destination and it is our destination most weekends!

Coastside Trail (gravel grinder)

Coastside Trail in Half Moon Bay defies categorization as a road or mountain tandem trail. Part dirt, part asphalt, it is smooth enough to ride a road bike on yet bumpy enough to prefer to ride it on a mountain tandem. A gravel grinder with larger tires may be a good compromise. If I had to choose, though? Mountain tandem, all day and twice on Sunday.

Coastside Trail actually starts north of Half Moon Bay in the tiny seaside village of Moss Beach. While not trying to plug *KNOCK KNOCK! It's Carmack!*, it remains true that if we have stayed at a B&B in California, you can be sure there is good riding close by! Moss Beach has Seal Cove Inn, at one point our favorite B&B. While Seal Cove Inn has lost its luster with us, Coastside Trail remains an absolute riot to ride on the bike.

This is due to the combination of surfaces (a literal mish-mash of road and dirt) combined with the scenery (a literal coastside trail in many parts) and topped with the end of the trail amongst the hoity-toity crowd at The Ritz-Carlton (with literal white-glove service). I imagine part of The Ritz-Carlton's approval to build

required an easement and extension of Coastside Trail. The first time you ride past the rich lunching on The Ritz-Carlton's patio, you will wonder if you had gotten lost. Once you realize you are still on Coastside Trail and it just happens to wend its way right by the pretty people dining, the return pass has you waving at them like lunatics. Some will even wave back. How could they not? You are on a tandem!

> The 16th hole is the end-point for the Coastside Trail. We will be back some day with Fred. (left)

> A small portion of the literal Coastside Trail. (right)

At nearly 40 miles round trip, it is not a tiring ride on a mountain tandem due to the relative flatness and smoothness of the trails and paths that make up Coastside Trail. There's also enough variation in sections of the route that you can ride it four or five times and not ride the same exact path. Combine that with zero crowds except around Redondo Beach and the beautiful scenery and this trail, all by itself, draws us back to the area time and again.

Mark Twain National Forest (mountain)

The Mark Twain National Forest is located throughout the southern half of Missouri. How did we find ourselves in the southern half of Missouri? See *KNOCK KNOCK! It's Carmack!*, available on Amazon, about our stay in **Suboptimal**.

We were there to ride with other tandem teams on our first AORTA. We packed up our Ventana (see **Coupling couplers**) and took it with us on our Southwest flight from LAX to St. Louis. Early the next morning I put it back together and we set out in search of other tandem teams to go ride in the Ozarks.

Up to the night before our first ride, it had been raining in the area, and a week before it had been flooding in the area. Were we back in SoCal with that much rain falling from the sky, we probably would have to stay off the trails for weeks. The soil is a bit different in the Ozarks, and it drains very well. The reason was more obvious once we got out on the trails.

Many tandems, heading into the Ozarks.

The trailbeds were mostly formed of small rock, smashed gravel or granite. This surface was not kind to tires, but gave us all the traction we needed and kept us mostly free of mud and goo. That was a big change from SoCal.

The other big change from SoCal was all the trees. We were riding through an honest forest. SoCal is all chaparral, with low scrub and the occasionally oak tree or Sycamore for something approaching shade. In the

Ozarks, the trails slalomed through tree trunks and we were shaded from the sun the majority of the time.

Cannot see the trail for the trees.

The pictures fail to show much trail definition; with the water abounding, green also abounded. On the bike, the trailbeds were obvious, even if our specific direction was not always clear. Riding in the Ozarks was eye-opening. While we had ridden in an actual forest in Bend, Oregon, it was nothing like the Ozarks. Riding with 15 other tandem teams made the whole thing all the more special.

Newbury Park Surf Loop (gravel grinder)

One of the new local rides that Fred, our **Co-Motion Java**, opened up is a road/dirt loop from our house in Newbury Park. From our door we can ride on backroads leading from Newbury Park to the Oxnard Plain, descending the remainder of the west end of the Santa Monica mountains on Potrero Road.

Potrero Road is all downhill from here.

Just past Channel Islands University (originally an insane asylum and the basis for the Eagles' song *Hotel California*) we make a left turn and ride through strawberry, artichoke, and sod farmland to the Pacific Ocean.

On the PCH, with Thornhill Broom sand hill in the distance. Look honey, dolphins!

At that point we make another left and head down a portion of Pacific Coast Highway between Naval Base Point Mugu and Sycamore Cove State Beach (see **Point Mugu State Park**). At that point, yes, another left into Point Mugu State Park, where we stop for a break. Refreshed, we take Sycamore Canyon Fireroad back home to Newbury Park. This is about a 35 mile ride that would have been uncomfortable (and much slower) on the Ventana.

Team Serles at the beach. It was a gray day, but a great ride. (right)

Cross Marin Trail (gravel grinder)

The Cross Marin Trail is a rails-to-trails path beginning at the intersection of Sir Francis Drake Blvd. and Point Reyes-Petaluma Road. Cross Marin Trail is a multi-use trail closed to vehicular traffic. It begins in a landscape of coastal scrub and it can be sunny and 85°F as you start your ride. After a mile or so you start to transition into forest, for the Cross Marin Trail parallels Lagunitas Creek as it cuts through our favorite campground - Samuel P. Taylor State Park.

By the time you hit Jewell trailhead (which heads up to Bolinas Ridge Trail, see the photo accompanying **Bittersweat tandem sales**) you are into pine trees galore, shade returns, and the temperature starts to drop. From the start and into the campground proper (approximately five miles) the surface is good-condition asphalt. By this time you will have transitioned from pine tree forest to full-on redwoods. The shade increases and the temperature drops some more.

As you pass south-east through the campground, the path turns to dirt fireroad, but stays mostly flat. The rises are mostly the various path bridges over Sir Frances Drake Blvd, which Cross Marin Trail finally ends at, about 5 miles south of the campground.

That does not end your ride, however. Quickly crossing Sir Frances Drake leads you to a gated entry for Marin Municipal Water District land and Lower Peters Dam Road. Keep to the left of Lagunitas Creek and the mixed-surface trail continues flat for about a half-mile. Then it kicks up as it climbs the face of Peters Dam, which holds back the Marin area freshwater supply of Shafter Lake.

We use this loop to shake off the cobwebs after driving seven hours to get here from SoCal. There are a wide variety of different routes the branch off Cross Marin. If you kept to the right side of Lagunitas Creek when entering Marin Municipal Water District land, you could climb Shafter Grade (warning, it is steep and loose!) and join Bolinas Ridge Trail. If you are on the dam itself, you can stay on the left and climb further into the forest. Ride long enough and you will end up at the top of Repack, the legendary trail that birthed mountain biking!

The water looks refreshing, but there is no swimming allowed in Shafter Lake. (right)

Get on your bike and ride! (following page)

Made in the USA
Coppell, TX
15 June 2020